Warren Upham, Mary Upham Kelley

Upham and Amherst, N.H., memories:

The genealogy and history of a branch of the Upham family

Warren Upham, Mary Upham Kelley

Upham and Amherst, N.H., memories:
The genealogy and history of a branch of the Upham family

ISBN/EAN: 9783337726690

Printed in Europe, USA, Canada, Australia, Japan

Cover: Foto ©ninafisch / pixelio.de

More available books at **www.hansebooks.com**

AND

AMHERST. N. H.,

Memories;

THE GENEALOGY AND HISTORY OF A BRANCH OF THE
UPHAM FAMILY.

―――――――――

*" Honor thy father and thy mother, that thy days may be long upon
the land which the Lord thy God giveth thee."*

―――――――――

By Mrs. Mary Upham Kelley
AND
Warren Upham.

―――――――――

PRIVATELY PRINTED:
MARCH 25, 1897.

CONTENTS.

———

OUR ANCESTRY AND KINDRED.

" Beneath those rugged elms, that yew tree's shade,
  Where heaves the turf in many a mould'ring heap,
  Each in his narrow cell for ever laid.
    The rude forefathers of the hamlet sleep.

" The breezy call of incense-breathing morn,
  The swallow twitt'ring from the straw-built shed.
  The cock's shrill clarion, or the echoing horn,
    No more shall rouse them from their lowly bed.

" For them no more the blazing hearth shall burn,
  Or busy housewife ply her evening care :
  No children run to lisp their sire's return.
    Or climb his knees the envied kiss to share."

INTRODUCTION.

The early records of our family name, and our ancestors to the third Phineas Upham, which are briefly presented in the following pages, have been derived from the research of others. The earliest publication tracing our name is a little book of 92 pages, published by Dr. Albert G. Upham, of Concord, N. H., in 1845, entitled "Notices of the Life of John Upham, the first Inhabitant of New England who bore that name: together with an Account of such of his Descendants as were the Ancestors of Hon. Nathaniel Upham, of Rochester, New Hampshire; with a short Sketch of the Life of the Latter." The latest and most complete register of our family history is by Capt. Frank Kidder Upham, a book of 573 pages, with numerous portraits, views of the old Upham homestead in Melrose. Mass., and of the ancient church of Bicton, England, and facsimiles of handwriting. This work, issued in 1892, is entitled "Upham Genealogy: the Descendants of John Upham, of Massachusetts, who came from England in 1635, and lived in Weymouth and Malden, embracing over five hundred heads of families, extending into the tenth generation."

An ancient Bible, which was owned by the third Phineas Upham. our grandfather's grandfather, containing a page of family records in his writing, another page written by our great-grandfather, and a third page by our grandfather, now owned by the junior author of this sketch, the Bible register written by our mother, records of subsequent dates carefully kept by our sister Lizzie, and still more recent names and dates, bring the story of our kindred onward to the present time.

Origin of the Name Upham.

The surname Upham is first found in records of Wiltshire, England, in 1208. About a hundred and fifty years earlier. however, during the reign of King Edward the Confessor (1042 to 1066), Upham was the name of a land estate, as noted in the Doomsday Book. It was probably formed by uniting the Anglo-Saxon words *Up*, high, and *ham*, a home, dwelling, or hamlet, meaning thus "the Home on the Hill." The name was in use before the battle of Hastings, but it seems uncertain whether our ancestor who first assumed this surname from his estate or village was of Saxon or of Norman origin.

Upham is now the name of a parish of Hampshire, England, in which Edward Young, the poet, was born in 1681. It is also the name of a village in Ireland, about a hundred miles southwest of Dublin.

Ancestors in England (1500–1635).

The earliest of our ancestors from whom a continuous line is traced to the present time was Richard Upham, who was living at Bicton, in Devonshire, England, in 1523. and died there in 1546.

His son, John Upham, of Eatenton in the parish of Bicton,

died in 1584, leaving a will by which his son Richard inherited his small farm.

This Richard Upham was the father of John and Sarah Upham, and of Joane (married to Robert Martin), who emigrated together to America in 1635, contrary to their father's wishes. They sailed, in a company numbering one hundred and six, led by Rev. Joseph Hull, from Weymouth, England, on the 20th day of March, 1635, and reached Boston on the 6th of May. Early in July, by direction of the General Court of the Massachusetts Bay colony, they settled in the town which, in affectionate remembrance of the port whence they sailed, was named Weymouth, on the south shore of the bay.

Maria, the mother in England, had died late in July of the preceding year, 1634, and in December, 1635, the father, Richard Upham, died. His will gave to " Sarah Uppam, my daughter in New England," five pounds, on the condition that within three years she should write to her sisters in England, the executrixes of the will, " that shee hath need of it." Greater disapproval is expressed in the next bequests : " Item. I give to John Uppam, my sonne in New England, if he come for it, five shillings. Item. I give to Joane Martin, my daughter, if shee come for it, five shillings." Doubtless many heartaches, both of the emigrants and of their father, had preceded this will, which was made on the 12th of December, 1635, just one week before his burial.

An inventory of Richard Upham's personal property, including household goods, farming tools, etc., with " one Bibell boke and other bokes," to the value of thirteen shillings, amounted in total to fifty-nine pounds and eleven shillings.

Our English Cousins.

The only brother of John Upham, the emigrant, was Thomas Upham, who succeeded his father on the farm at Bicton. His descendants bearing the name Upham are somewhat numerous in Bristol, Exeter, and elsewhere in southern England. To one of these descendants, William Reynell-Upham of Bristol, we are greatly indebted for his researches, by which the English home of John Upham, and some of the Upham lines of descent in England, were ascertained and published in 1892, as a supplement, in the American " Upham Genealogy."

1. JOHN UPHAM (1597–1681), EMIGRANT TO AMERICA IN 1635.

The emigrant, John Upham, from whom all bearing the Upham name in the United States and Canada are descendants, was born in 1597, in Bicton parish, England, on the river Otter and near the seacoast of southeastern Devonshire. He was married at Bicton on November 1st, 1626, to Elizabeth Slade; emigrated to Weymouth in 1635; removed to Malden, Mass., in 1648, or within a year or two later; and died in Malden, February 25th, 1681.

Dr. Albert G. Upham, in the book before noticed, wrote of our first forefather in New England as follows:

The character of John Upham appears in a clear light. . . . At the age of 38, within fifteen years of the first settlement of Plymouth, he sought an asylum for himself and family in this country. We thus see him in early manhood exhibiting his energy of character, and the clearness and vigor of his intellectual powers, in the act of resigning kindred, friends and country, for God and liberty. In this great act his spirit bears witness of itself.

In addition to this, we find him, on his arrival here, approved by his countrymen, as he was the same year chosen a delegate to their highest Assembly, and for six different sessions continued their representative, when fearless piety, integrity and wisdom, were regarded as essential to office. On his removal to Malden, thirteen years afterward, he became at once, and continued through life, a leading citizen of that town, and was repeatedly elected to various offices in their gift. The General Assembly also manifest a corresponding confidence in him, by appointing him six times Commissioner to settle the lesser legal matters of Weymouth and Malden.

During the short period that the town records are extant, it appears that he was eight years selectman, and three years moderator of the town meetings. He was a commissioner to treat with the Indians, and was a pioneer, not only in the first settlement of Weymouth and Malden, but actively interested in the settlement of Worcester.

It will likewise be seen, from the frequency with which he was called upon to settle estates, and to manage the affairs of widows and orphans, that he was esteemed a man of carefulness and kindness in the discharge of these important trusts.

Finally, the church, in a highly religious community, setteth the seal of her testimony upon him, by selecting him for the office of Deacon which office he held for at least twenty-four years.

His sons he educated for the service of his country: the one became a minister of the gospel, the other an officer in the army. In all his domestic relations there is reason to believe him a man esteemed and beloved.

Nature seems to have endowed him with a vigorous constitution: for, at the age of 83, but a few months before his decease, he discharged the laborious duties of moderator, thus showing that he enjoyed at that time full activity of mind and body.

The children of John Upham and his wife, Elizabeth Slade, were John, Nathaniel, and Elizabeth, born in England, and coming with their parents to America in the Hull company; and Phineas, Mary, and Priscilla, born in New England. Phineas, meaning "the peace of God," first appears among our family names, so far as is known, in being given to the earliest born in the New World, probably to commemorate the feelings of peace and thankfulness for safe arrival here. It was borne in succession by three generations of our ancestral line.

2. PHINEAS UPHAM (1635-1676), DYING OF A WOUND RE- CEIVED IN KING PHILIP'S WAR.

Phineas, born in 1635 (probably in May or June), married Ruth Wood, April 14th, 1658; served in 1675 as a lieutenant in the war against the Indian chief, King Philip, and was wound- ed in the battle of the great Swamp Fort, December 19th; and died, as the result of his wound, in the following October, 1676. Dr. Albert G. Upham says of him:

It would seem that Lieutenant Upham possessed in a high degree that genius of enterprise so characteristic of his father. Worcester, called in his will "Consugameg, alias Lydbury," a fair and beautiful town, owes its foundation in no small degree, as it clearly appears, to his activity and energy.

In the military service of his country it is manifest that he was es- teemed a meritorious and efficient officer, having, in his short career, at- tracted the favorable notice of the government, and been once associated with an officer of the Plymouth Colony in command of a highly hazard- ous expedition into the enemy's country.

In battle Lieutenant Upham exhibited the character of a brave man and patriot, purchasing with mortal wounds the palm of victory; and the government was not unmindful of his great sacrifice, but bore tes- timony upon her records " to the long and good services he did to the country, and the great loss sustained by his friends in his death."

Though cut off in early manhood, he gave to the world full assurance of a man to whom each succeeding year would have brought new and more abundant honor.

The children of Lieutenant Phineas Upham and his wife, Ruth Wood, were as follows, all being born in Malden:

Phineas, b. May 22, 1659; d. Oct., 1720.
Nathaniel, b. 1661; d. Nov. 11, 1717.
Ruth, b. 1664; d. Dec. 8, 1676.
John, b. Dec. 9, 1666; d. June 9, 1733.
Elizabeth. m. Samuel Green, Oct. 28, 1691.
Thomas. b. 1668; d. Nov. 26, 1735.
Richard, b. 1675; d. May 18, 1734.

The three sisters of Lieutenant Phineas were each married, and they are doubtless represented by many 'descendants in the United States and Canada. As they do not bear the name Upham, they are not traced in our published family genealogy. The brothers John and Nathaniel left no descendants, and therefore all of our family name in this country are the children not only of John, the emigrant, but also of the first Phineas Upham. His sons, however, all married and left children. We are descendants of his eldest son, whose family record is here given fully.

Descendants of Nathaniel (b. 1661) are now living in Royalston, Templeton, and other towns of Massachusetts, and in New York and Ohio.

John (b. 1666) has many descendants in Sturbridge and other towns of Massachusetts, and in Vermont, among whom was Hon. William Upham (1792-1853), during twelve years United States Senator from Vermont. Others of this branch are Major John H. Upham (1841-) of Duluth, Minn., and his cousin, Gov. William H. Upham (1841-), of Marshfield, Wis.

Descendants of Thomas (b. 1668), in the third generation, settled in Cape Town, South Africa. Among his other descendants are families in Canton and Stoughton, Mass.; Capt. Frank K. Upham (1841-), genealogist, of the United States Army; and Isaac Upham (1837-), of San Francisco, California.

From Richard (b. 1675) came Hon. Nathan Upham and others in Drayton and Grafton. North Dakota.

3. THE SECOND PHINEAS UPHAM (1659-1720).

Phineas, the grandson of the emigrant John, born May 22, 1659, married Mary Mellins (or Mellen) in 1682 or 1683; was one of the selectmen of Malden, 1692 to 1696, again 1701 to 1704, and in later years; town treasurer, 1697 to 1701; five times representative to the General Court of Massachusetts, 1701 to 1718; four times moderator of the Malden town meetings, 1711 to 1717; and a deacon of the church from 1710 to his death in 1720.

The children of the second Phineas and his wife Mary were:

Phineas, b. June 10, 1682; d. probably in 1766.

Mary, b. 1685; d. Aug. 20. 1687.

James, b. 1687; date of death unknown, after 1725.

Mary, b. 1689; m. John Griffin, May 28, 1713.

Ebenezer, b. probably 1691 or 1692; d. probably 1760.

Jonathan, b. 1694; d. May 16, 1750.

William, b. Oct. 30, 1697; date of death after 1743.

Elizabeth, b. 1699 or 1700; m. Jonathan Dowse, Jr., May 19, 1726; d. June 19, 1730.

James, of this family, was the great-grandfather of Hon. Benjamin F. Wade (1800-1878), who during eighteen years was United States Senator from Ohio.

4. The third Phineas Upham (1682-1766).

This was our grandfather's grandfather. His family Bible, in which he wrote the registry of his children, was used by our grandfather for his daily reading. After his death it was owned by our brother George, by whom, in his will, it was given to Warren Upham.

The third Phineas, being the last of this name in our line of descent, was born June 10, 1682; and married Tamzen (Thomasin) Hill, Nov. 23, 1703. About that time, or earlier, he built the house on Upham hill in North Malden (now Melrose) which (with subsequent enlargement) is still standing, and is occupied by his descendant, Orne Upham. He was at various times one of the selectmen, an assessor, and moderator of the town meetings.

Dr. Albert G. Upham wrote in 1845:

Mr. John Edmonds, of Malden, an old soldier, now 89 years of age, informs me that when a boy he often saw Phineas Upham. He states that he was of medium height; his hair abundant, but of a pure white, and his costume that of his time, viz.—breeches, cocked hat, etc. He used to walk about the village with the assistance of an ivory-headed cane, and he had a favorite seat beneath a wide-spreading tree, where he was often seen reposing. He "valued himself," says Mr. Edmonds, "on his French blood."

The children of this third Phineas Upham and his wife, Tamzen Hill, were:

Tabitha. b. Dec. 11, 1704; m. Daniel Newhall, 1728.
Mary, b. March 5, 1706; m. Capt. Daniel Goff, of Boston, 1740.
Phineas, b. Jan. 14, 1708; d. July 17, 1738.
Sarah, b. May 31, 1709; d. Sept. 23, 1709.
Timothy, b. Aug. 29, 1710; d. July 3, 1781.
Zebediah, b. March 13, 1712; d. April 28, 1712.
Tamzen, b. May 5, 1713; d. June 14, 1713.
Isaac, b. July 31, 1714; d. probably in 1792.
Jabez, b. Jan. 3, 1717; d. Nov. 4, 1760.
Amos. b. Sept. 29, 1718; d. Jan. 23, 1786.
Tamzen, b. May 21, 1720; m. Jonathan Wiley, of Lynn, 1750.
Sarah, b. Oct. 17, 1721; m. Benjamin Rice, of Brookfield, Mass., 1744.
Jacob, b. April 30, 1723; d. Sept. 30, 1775.

In this family, the fourth Phineas Upham (b. 1708) was the great-grandfather of Ralph Waldo Emerson (1803-1882).

Timothy (b. 1710) was the father of Rev. Timothy Upham (1748-1811), of Deerfield, N. H., whose son Nathaniel (1774-1829) was representative in Congress from New Hampshire (1817-1823) and was the father of Prof. Thomas C. Upham (1799-1872), of Bowdoin College, Maine, and of Judge Nathaniel G. Upham (1801-1869), of Concord, N. H., and Dr. Albert G. Upham (1819-1847), the author of the earliest publication on our family history. By another line of descent, Timothy (b. 1710) was the great-grandfather of Rev. James Upham, of Chelsea, Mass., one of the editors of the Youth's Companion.

From Isaac Upham (b. 1714) is descended, in the fourth generation, Mr. Henry P. Upham, of St. Paul, Minn., who aided greatly in the compilation and publication of the Upham Genealogy.

From Jabez Upham (b. 1717), of Brookfield, Mass., are descended many of our name in New Brunswick, where his son Jabez (1747-1834) was a pioneer settler of the town of Upham, named in his honor; also Rev. Charles Wentworth Upham (1802-1875), of Salem, Mass., author and representative in Congress; and Hon. George B. Upham (1768-1848), of Claremont, N. H., and his son, Dr. Jabez Baxter Upham (1820-), of Boston, and later of New York City.

Amos (b. 1718) was the father of Phineas Upham (1744-1815), who settled in the north part of Amherst, N. H., where some of his descendants are still living.

5. JACOB UPHAM (1723-1775), OUR GREAT-GRANDFATHER.

The name Jacob appeared earliest in our family as given by John (b. 1666), a son of the first Phineas, to his youngest son, born in 1719, who died in infancy. Four years later this name, most characteristic of our branch of the Upham family, was given by the third Phineas to his youngest son, the last of his thirteen children. He was born in Malden, April 30, 1723; and married Rebecca Burnap, in Reading, Mass., Jan. 19, 1748, who was born Jan. 18, 1727, and died March 14, 1779. He lived in Reading, where his name was enrolled in a list of voters in 1771, and among the pew-owners of the First Parish Meeting-House. He died Sept. 30, 1775; and his will was proved in 1779.

The children of this first Jacob Upham and his wife Rebecca were:

Rebecca, b. Dec. 2, 1748; d. April 1, 1749.

Rebecca, b. Jan. 9, 1750; d. March 10, 1777.

Sarah, b. March 16, 1753; d. July 28, 1753.

Sarah, b. July 17, 1754; d. May 24, 1775.

Mary, b. May 2, 1757; m. William Tarbox, of North Reading, Mass., April 4, 1780; d. Oct. 18, 1820.

Tamzen, b. Sept. 5, 1759; d. Jan. 26, 1822.

Ruth, b. Jan. 18, 1763; d. March 21, 1810.

Jacob, b. May 16, 1766; d. April 1, 1849.

6. THE SECOND JACOB UPHAM (1766-1849), OUR GRANDFATHER.

A cousin of our grandfather, the son Phineas of his uncle Amos Upham, had removed to Amherst, N. H., probably about twenty-five years earlier than our grandfather, who was born in Reading, Mass., May 17, 1766, married Sarah Pratt, of Reading, Nov. 17, 1791, and removed to Amherst in 1792. He lived on the farm then purchased until his death, April 1, 1849. His first wife, Sarah Pratt, our grandmother, was born April 20, 1759, and died Nov. 17, 1826. She was the sixth child in the family of Daniel Pratt, of Reading, who was born July 22, 1725; was married in 1747; and died June 22, 1795. Our grandfather's second wife, Sarah Whittemore, of Charlestown, Mass., to whom he was married April 15, 1827, was born July 25, 1775, and died April 28, 1849.

The children of the second Jacob Upham and his wife, Sarah Pratt, were one born, not living, Sept. 17, 1792; Sally,

born March 22, 1794, who died March 17, 1796; and Jacob, born
Oct. 29, 1798. There were no children by the second marriage.

7. THE THIRD JACOB UPHAM (1798-1859), OUR FATHER.

On the home farm in Amherst, N. H., and probably in the
same room where all his ten children first saw the light, our
father was born Oct. 29, 1798. He was married, by Rev. Cyrus Peirce, Nov. 20, 1822, in North Reading, Mass., to Sarah
Hayward of that town. Her parents were William Hayward
(b. Aug. 18, 1761: d. July 30, 1829) and his wife, Dorcas
Townsend (b. May 29, 1768; d. June 8, 1853). They lived on
the farm, nearly two miles east of the village of North Reading, which afterward was the home of her youngest brother,
Andrew Hayward (1811-1880), and now of his son, Martin L.
Hayward, who has built a larger house very near the old site.
Two others of her brothers were Aaron Hayward (1794-1879)
and Josiah Hayward (1801-1874), both of Salem, Mass., where
their children, our cousins, and their children, still reside.
Our mother was born Aug. 31, 1804, and died March 17, 1891,
in Nashua, N. H., to which city she removed, with our sister
Lizzie, in the autumn of 1871. Our father died of consump-
tion Oct. 14, 1859. One of his sons said of him :

He was born, lived, and died, on the same farm at Amherst that had
been his father's. He was an honest, industrious, cheerful, hopeful and
contented Christian man, unambitious for rank or wealth. In appear-
ance, slender and rather tall; somewhat delicate in health during the
greater part of his life. In religious faith he was a Congregationalist,
and in political preference a Whig—later a Republican; but he never
held, nor aspired to any conspicuous office. He brought up a large family, nine of whom reached mature years and remembered their father
and mother with sincere love and gratitude.

The children of our parents were:
Jacob Burnap, b. Jan. 4, 1824; d. Dec. 19, 1891.
Sarah Tamzan, b. Feb. 7, 1826; d. Nov. 16, 1860.
Mary, b. March 25, 1827: now living in the village of Salem Depot,
N. H.
Emily Dorcas, b. July 30, 1829; d. June 20, 1863.
Susan, b. April 14, 1832; now living in the village of Troy, N. H.
John Henry, b. Nov. 21, 1835; now living in Merrimack, N. H.
Ruth Elizabeth, b. Oct. 18, 1838: d. July 20, 1888.
Jesse Hayward, b. Feb. 19, 1841; d. March 3, 1841.
George William, b. April 23, 1842; d. Feb. 12, 1883.
Warren, b. March 8, 1850; now living in St. Paul, Minn.

We are in the eighth generation of American Uphams, and are accordingly designated in this record as 8a, 8b, etc., with children and grandchildren in the ninth and tenth generations.

8a.   Jacob Burnap Upham, our Brother.

Our oldest brother, the fourth in succession of this Christian name, was born Jan. 4, 1824, and married Mary E. Chapin, of Antrim, N. H., Aug. 31, 1871, who was born May 12, 1835, and died Nov. 11, 1874. He was again married Nov. 4, 1875, to Sarah F. Converse, of Amherst, who was born Sept. 15, 1845. He died very suddenly of heart failure, Dec. 19, 1891. From 1871 to his death he owned and lived on the old homestead in Amherst, N. H., which is still the home of his widow. His children, two by the first and one by the second wife, are:

Mary Bertha, b. Aug. 15, 1872; living at the old home.
Ernest Jacob, b. July 17, 1874; d. Aug. 15, 1875.
Charles Jacob, b. Aug. 16, 1876; living at the old home.

8b.   Sarah Tamzan Upham Vose, our Sister.

The second name of this sister was given, in accordance with our grandfather's wish, in memory of his sister; and his mother's surname had become, similarly, our brother Jacob's second name. Sister Sarah was born Feb. 7, 1826; was married in Nashua, N. H., by Rev. Austin Richards, to Samuel H. Vose, Nov. 6, 1849; lived in the village of Salem, N. H.; and died there Nov. 16, 1860. Mr. Vose was afterward married, Aug. 26, 1862, to Maria H. Hills, and lived in Nashua, N. H., where he died Jan. 9, 1895. There were no children by the second marriage, and his widow died Dec. 29, 1895. The children of our sister Sarah were:

Elizabeth Sarah Vose, b. Oct. 27, 1850; d. Feb. 25, 1870.
Josephine Vose, b. Aug. 16, 1853; d. July 4, 1879.
Ellen Vose, b. Sept. 29, 1855; d. May 23, 1856.

8c.   Mary Upham Kelley

Was born March 25, 1827; was married in Amherst, by Rev. J. G. Davis, to Gilman D. Kelley, Nov. 25, 1847; and now lives at Salem Depot, N. H.

Gilman D. Kelley was in the seventh generation of this family name in America, as is learned, for the earlier part of the

record, from Morrison's *History of Windham, N. H.* His
emigrant ancestor, John Kelley, came with his family in a
company of seventy emigrants from Newbury, Berkshire, England, in 1635, and settled in Newbury, Mass. He died about
1612, leaving one son, John, who was a prosperous farmer in
Newbury. From one of his sons, Abiel, born Dec. 12, 1672,
came three successive descendants, each bearing the name
Richard Kelley. The first of these was born in Newbury Oct.
24, 1697; his son Richard was born Nov. 7, 1737, and lived in
Salem, N. H., being one of the founders of this town; and his
son, the third Richard, was born July 19, 1783. This Richard
Kelley, and his wife, Betsey Webster, were the parents of
Gilman Dinsmore Kelley, who was born Jan. 24, 1824, married to Mary Upham, as before noted, in 1847; and died Aug.
9, 1884.

Their children are:

Richard Gilman Kelley, b. Nov. 2, 1818; d. April 6, 1850.
Benjamin Payson Kelley, b. Feb. 9, 1851; living in Salem, N. H.
Marietta Kelley, b. Aug. 23, 1852; d. Oct. 17, 1852.
Emily Maria Kelley, b. Jan. 15, 1854; living in Salem, N. H.
Sarah Esther Kelley, b. May 2, 1861; living at Salem Depot, N. H.
Louisa Betsey Kelley, b. June 22, 1862; d. Jan. 18, 1863.
Jacob William Kelley, b. Sept. 14, 1864; living in Salem, N. H.

9CA. THE CHILDREN OF BENJAMIN P. KELLEY and his wife,
Maggie C. Farr, to whom he was married in Methuen, Mass.,
Sept. 25, 1877, are:

Arthur Gilman Kelley, b. July 17, 1879.
Lena Ardelle Kelley, b. Oct. 12, 1881.
Eva Viola Kelley, b. Jan. 25, 1885.
Mildred Kelley, b. Sept. 16, 1891.

9CB. EMILY MARIA KELLEY (USUALLY CALLED EMMA) was
married to William Hunt, Oct. 22, 1881; no children.

9CC. SARAH ESTHER KELLEY (USUALLY CALLED ESTHER) was
married Nov. 16, 1880, to Edward Farr, of Methuen, who was
a brother of Benjamin's wife. He lost his life at the burning
of his barn, Feb. 23, 1886.

Their children are:

George Closson Farr, b. Nov. 6, 1881.
Benjamin Edward Farr, b. Sept. 20, 1886.

9CD. THE CHILDREN OF JACOB WILLIAM KELLEY (usually
called Will) and his wife, Alice H. Goodwin, of Lebanon,

Maine, to whom he was married in Nashua. N. H., by Rev.
Cyrus Richardson, June 5, 1889, are:
  Bertha Goodwin Kelley, b. April 8, 1890.
  Ruth Upham Kelley, b. Oct. 11, 1891.
  Mabel Frances Kelley, b. Jan. 27, 1894.
  Rachel Hayward Kelley, b. April 27, 1896.

8d.   EMILY DORCAS UPHAM BABCOCK, OUR SISTER.

The second name of this sister was given in memory of our
mother's mother. Emily was born July 30, 1829; and was
married, by Rev. Asaph Merriam, to his son, Lucius Bolles
Merriam, May 28, 1851. He died June 17, 1853. She was
again married, also by Rev. Asaph Merriam, to Henry E. Babcock, of Bolton, Mass., Feb. 13, 1858; and they lived in Bolton,
where she died June 20, 1863. Mr. Babcock was again married, and is still living in Bolton. Emily's children, one by
each husband, were:
  Emma Marietta Merriam, b. May 7, 1852; d. June 10, 1885.
  Lizzie Sarah Babcock, b. Nov. 21, 1858; living in Bolton, Mass.

9da.   EMMA MARIETTA MERRIAM was married in Nashua, N.

H., Jan. 4, 1871, by Rev. Frederick Alvord, to Alonzo F. Gould,
of that city, where they lived and where Emma died, June
10, 1885. Mr. Gould was again married, and died in Nashua,
leaving a widow, Jan. 13, 1890. Emma's children are:
  Lucius Richard Gould, b. March 17, 1872; went several years ago to
Louisiana, and afterward to Montana.
  Warren Franklin Gould, b. Nov. 5, 1874.
  Benjamin Auld Gould, b. Jan. 25, 1877.
  Jacob Emerton Gould, b. Oct. 22, 1878.
    These three are living in or near Nashua, N. H.
  George Wilbur Hayward Gould, b. Nov. 21, 1882; d. July 16, 1883.

9db.   LIZZIE SARAH BABCOCK was married to William J.

Woodworth, Jan. 22, 1880. Their children are:
  Ralph Bowditch Woodworth, b. Aug. 18, 1881; d. June 27, 1882.
  Albert Shepard Woodworth, b. Sept. 30, 1882.
  Zella Frances Woodworth, b. Oct. 15, 1883.
  Louise Emily Woodworth, b. Aug. 1, 1889; d. Aug. 14, 1889.
  Dorothy Woodworth, b. Nov. 22, 1896.

8e.   SUSAN UPHAM LOWE, OUR SISTER,

Was born April 14, 1832; and was married, in our home, by
Rev. J. G. Davis, to David Perkins Lowe (usually called Perkins), of Amherst, June 14, 1855. Mr. Lowe was born March

31, 1816. in Fitchburg, Mass., and was a widower, with a son,
William P. Lowe, who now lives with our sister and family.
in Troy, N. H.   During several years they lived in the village
of Amherst; but in 1861 removed to Troy, purchasing a hill
farm about one and a half miles southeast of the village, where
Mr. Lowe built a new house, which was their home until his
death, July 20, 1894.   Subsequently our sister has lived
mostly in Troy village, but still retains the ownership and care
of the farm.   Her children are:

  Ambry Delia Lowe, b. Aug. 21, 1857; living in Troy.
  David Brainerd Lowe. b. April 16, 1861; living in Somerville, Mass.
  Susan Pauline Lowe, b. Feb. 21, 1873; living in Troy.

9EB.   DAVID BRAINERD LOWE was married to Florence Belle
Burnham, of the Roxbury District, Boston, Mass., April 9,
1890.   Their child, Florence Crystal Brainerd Lowe, was born
April 27, 1891.

8F.   JOHN HENRY UPHAM, OUR BROTHER,

Was born Nov. 21, 1835; and married Catherine E. Colburn
(usually called Katie), of Merrimack, N. H., April 22, 1862.
They lived in Amherst successively on the first farm and on
the second farm east of the old homestead, and afterward on
the Colburn homestead in Merrimack.   Their children are:

  Charles Henry, b. March 27, 1863; living in Merrimack.
  George Foster, b. Sept. 21, 1865; living in Merrimack.
  Osgood Fifield. b. July 29, 1869; living with his father.

9FA.   CHARLES HENRY UPHAM was married to Isabel Wood-
ward (usually called Bell), of Merrimack, June 24, 1890.
They live in Merrimack, nearly a mile south of Thornton's
Ferry.   Their child, Harlan Willis, was born March 4, 1892.

9FB.   GEORGE FOSTER UPHAM was married to Ella L. S.
Hodgman, of Bedford, N. H., Sept. 23, 1891.   They live on
the old Carlton farm, the most westerly in Merrimack on the
road to Amherst, where George has built a new house and
barn.

8G.   RUTH ELIZABETH UPHAM, OUR SISTER.

According to her preference, this sister was usually called
Lizzie.   With great love and constancy of devotion, she cared
for our mother during her declining years, therefore remaining unmarried.   She died in Nashua, N. H., July 20, 1888.

8ɪ. George William Upham, our Brother.

Was born April 23, 1842; and married Sarah A. Buss (b. Oct. 6, 1844), of Temple, N. H., May 2, 1867. They lived in Amherst, and afterward in Nashua, where he died Feb. 12, 1883, and his wife April 12, 1883. Their children are:

Edmund Warren, b. March 18, 1868; living in Dover, N. H.
Herbert George, b. Feb. 4, 1874; living in Merrimack, N. H.

9ɪᴀ. Edmund Warren Upham married in Fitchburg. Mass.. June 6, 1894, Myrtle Maud Harvey (b. at Derby Line, Vt., June 10, 1874). Their child, Bernice Maud, was born Nov. 8, 1896.

8ᴊ. Warren Upham

Was born March 8, 1850; and was married in Minneapolis, Minn., by Rev. John L. Scudder, to Addie Minerva Bixby, of Aurora, Minn., Oct. 22, 1885. They lived in Somerville, Mass., 1885 to 1893; and are now living in St. Paul, Minn. Their only child, a daughter Pearl, was born in Aurora, Minn., Sept. 26, 1887, not living.

Addie Bixby Upham was born in Aurora, Feb. 5, 1861. Her father was John Bixby, who was born in Moretown, Vt., Jan. 28, 1815, and died in Aurora, Jan. 15, 1890. He was one of the first pioneers of Steele county, Minnesota, emigrating thither from Vermont in 1855. His parents were Theophilus Bixby, born in Westford, Mass., July 1, 1781, and Anna, his wife, born in Groton, Mass., June 3, 1778. Addie's mother was Malinda Polly Schagel, who was born April 10, 1817, in Chatham, a town of the Province of Quebec adjoining the north side of the Ottawa river; was married to John Bixby, in Cabot, Vt., Feb. 2, 1840; and died in Aurora, Minn.. July 26, 1895. Her parents were Jacob Schagel, born April 14. 1786, and Polly Noble, born Jan. 26, 1793, the date of their marriage being Jan. 26, 1809. They lived in Chatham, P. Q.. about halfway between Montreal and Ottawa.

W.

OUR GRANDPARENTS.

" Children's children are the crown of old men; and the glory of children are their fathers."

One of my earliest recollections is the return of my paternal grandparents from a visit in Massachusetts. They went with my father's horse and wagon. Covered carriages had not then come into common use. Occasionally some of the wealthy and aristocratic rode in chaises—covered vehicles having only two wheels. Such now are rarely seen. There was not a railroad at that time anywhere in New England.

Our grandfather was married twice. The wife he then had was not our father's own mother, but a second wife, married in 1827, a few weeks after my birth. For their home a new house was built only a few rods from our father's. So near were the two houses that we commingled nearly as much as though all under one roof.

On their return home they brought to each of us children a present. I am quite sure that each had one, though I have entirely forgotten what the other presents were. But I remember distinctly the gift they made me. It was a medium-sized doll, in full dress. How delighted I was! Yet I was rather piqued because mother did not lavish encomiums on my new treasure. She laughed, and said it ought to have little feet, and shoes, and hands. But I did not care, as it had legs with knee and hip joints; also arms with elbow and shoulder joints. To be sure, all Dolly's limbs were made of narrow strips of wood, flat as any school ma'am's ruler, with no pretense of the rounded form of the natural model, the extremities being cut square off! Consequently the hand was not seen below the frill of the sleeve; nor the foot beneath the long, full skirts.

I was probably then between three and four years old,—so very young that I have no vivid remembrance of the conversation of the family. But, from what I recollect of it, I suppose that grandfather considered their visit the proper time to ascertain, if possible, what had become of the property left by his wife's father, whose name was John Whittemore. He died when she was only three years old. Her mother's death preceded his. They lived and died in Charlestown, Mass., leaving their little daughter, without brother or sister, alone in the world. That her father was a wealthy man was learned from a neighbor in Amherst, Mrs. William Melendy, who was herself a native of Charlestown, and well acquainted with its history; but grandfather did not succeed in securing any of the property.

When young, dear grandma was moved about from place to place; and when grown she worked in families and in that way earned a livelihood, never once suspecting, till near the time grandpa married her, that she ought to have been an heiress. Poor girl! Though not in abject poverty, she was not favored with privileges peculiarly gratifying to one aspiring to usefulness and honor. Her childhood was spent mostly in Charlestown, Boston, and Framingham, Mass. I once asked her how she came to be living in New Hampshire; she answered, laconically, "I came to take care of your grandpa." How very short her time when that work was done!

Grandfather was a fine looking old gentleman, tall and erect, not corpulent, but with broad shoulders and well-knit frame. His countenance and bearing were mild; yet they expressed firmness and decision, and gave evidence of stability of character. He and grandma were alike in humility and devotion. Each loved God and his service, and sought to promote the enlargement of his kingdom and glory, by holy living, and by helping others to do right, believing that righteousness and happiness ever must be closely allied.

Grandpa was a Congregationalist. So were my father and mother. Grandma was a Calvinistic Baptist, and attended the church services of that denomination; and grandpa's kindness and Christlikeness were manifest in his respect and regard for her religious views, her church, church people, and pastor. There was no Baptist church, during my childhood, in my home town, but there was in the neighboring village of Milford; and when grandma was well she highly enjoyed the opportunity of going there to worship. Grandpa used to go with her, and sometimes one of us children went with them. We were all the grandchildren they had, as father was an only child. He would have had a sister, but the prattling voice and pattering feet were silenced previous to his birth: and a little grave had hidden from sight the dearest treasure of that happy home. Yet amid their sorrow the bereaved parents could dry their tear-dimmed eyes, and soothe their aching hearts, in the sure belief that their little one had exchanged earth for heaven.

One rather bleak Sabbath in late autumn, I rode with them to the meeting at Milford, sitting in a small chair, in the front part of a one-seated carriage, pushed back as far as possible between the knees of the aged couple. A strong wind was blowing from the northwest, and before we had traveled half of the distance it seemed to pierce us through and through. Grandma took from her bear-skin muff a silk handkerchief, and, handing it to me, said, "Hold it against your face." I gladly obeyed: and could now designate very nearly the place on the road where we then were. Whether the handkerchief was white or colored I have forgotten, but well remember the softness of the silk and the warmth it imparted to my half-frozen cheeks.

When attending his own church, grandpa sat in a pew which in all probability he bought when a young man. It was a square pew in the "old meeting-house," with several seats which had hinges and were turned up at prayer time to give more standing-room; and when put down they made a terrible clatter. My father and his family also occupied the same pew. In 1837 this ancient church in the village of Amherst (more frequently called "Amherst Plain") was removed to its present site and was remodeled. With more recent changes, it is still, after an existence of a hundred and twenty-five years, the convenient and beautiful Congregational house of worship.

Grandpa loved the Sabbath and all its hallowed associations. He also enjoyed the week-day social meetings. These were often in the afternoon, with all ages attending, children, parents, and grandparents. Would that the mothers of to-day took with them their children when going to maternal, missionary, and other religious meetings! If this was their habitual practice, would they not gain much in several ways? They would know where their children were, what they were doing, and the influences brought to bear upon their plastic, susceptible minds.

Environment and companionships influence and develop character. In New England, sixty years ago, several generations often lived together. This necessitated considerable acceding to the wishes of others; else the household would have been inharmonious. As I look back to my childhood home, I remember no bickerings or disputes. Each one was interested for all the others. The children were taught to reverence the aged, and little ones to yield to superiors.

It was no tiresome walk to go from our house to grandpa's. The path between was well worn and often trod. We were like one family, yet so separate that each had right and title to certain possessions. Formerly grandpa owned the farm, but when father was of age he gave him a deed of it. Father agreed, by written contract, to furnish him each year with a stipulated sum of money, also a specified amount of wood, corn, rye, oats, and potatoes, and an opportunity to keep two cows. Father was to pasture the cows, and to feed them in winter, there being only one barn on the farm; and he was to furnish a horse and carriage for riding. As grandpa had opportunity, he was to assist in doing the work of the farm.

Once, when there was snow and ice, grandpa slipped and fell on his way to or from the barn, putting his shoulder out of joint. The accident proved quite serious, and for a long time prevented him from milking. Some years later he was sick for months, so that it was thought he could not recover; but he did, and lived about ten years in comparatively good health, although feeble and with impaired memory. He would remember the prices of the years gone by, but entirely forget that farm produce was at that time much higher. During those later years his work was confined mostly to planting his garden, of which he and grandma took the principal care. It was in a little field which formed the northwestern corner of the farm, enclosed by stone walls on three sides and on the west by woods.

Grandma was quite small, with pretty features, dark brown

hair, and very white, fair skin. She must have been handsome when young. She was several years younger than grandfather and was more fond of society. She called on her friends and neighbors often, and liked to visit. Having always delicate health, she occasionally suffered from nervous prostration, and would then lie in bed several days or even weeks in succession. My first experience in nursing was at those times. Day and night for weeks I staid at their house to wait on her and grandpa. Love lightened my labor and made gentle each ministration! Grandma enjoyed being read to, and, child as I then was, I delighted in reading to her. They had not an abundance of books, yet more than most families.

I well remember that grandfather spent much time in reading the Bible. Hours together he studied its contents with pleasure. Doubtless his fervor in prayer was the result of long seeking to walk in the Christian way. To this day his earnest and importunate petitions, mingled with thanksgiving and praise, are an inspiration and help to me, drawing heavenward.

He was interested in the political affairs of the country, and voted with the Democratic party of that time. He was opposed to intoxicating drinks, war, and slavery. I remember hearing him speak many times of watching the trend of transpiring events, and, almost with prophetic vision, denounce the wall he could see rising between the rich and poor, between employers and employees. His sympathies were sufficiently broad to extend to all.

In winter evenings some of us children used frequently to spend an hour or two in grandpa's house with them, before a blazing fire, eating apples, popcorn, and nuts, and listening to old-time stories. But we always left early so as not to interfere with their usual hour for retiring, which was between eight and nine o'clock. They believed in having an abundance of sleep, and consequently did not hasten to rise early. They were not people of haste, or waste; neither did they clutch with miserly grasp the honest reward of industry and economy, but gave liberally, according to circumstances and opportunity.

Grandfather and grandmother, though not very infirm, seemed to my young mind much older than persons of that age now do. I often wonder if I seem as old to my grandchildren as they did to me! Until I was married I was much with them. They were interested in all the affairs connected with our family, and received with friendliness and pleasure the stranger who came wooing. They were guests at the wedding, and their genial presence and affability added much to the enjoyment of the occasion. After witnessing the ceremony, they, by hearty shaking of hands, congratulations, and the expression of good wishes, showed unmistakably their cordiality.

The next morning my husband and I departed for our new home, and though in late autumn the day was balmy and delightful. From that time forward, I think that I saw them only once, which, if I recollect rightly, was in the following February. About one year later their days were numbered. Grandfather died the first day of April, 1849, and grandmother the twenty-eighth of the same month. She was apparently well when he died, but a cold contracted the day of his funeral culminated in pneumonia and produced her death. Their graves, marked by tablets, are in the cemetery east of Amherst common, near the entrance.

The close of life came to each without long illness. Grandmother had dreaded the hour of dissolution; but, as it drew near, our mother said to her, "You cannot be with us much longer. How do you feel in view of death?" She looked up with a sweet smile, and said, " Happy! happy! happy! " emphasizing the word more and more; and then quietly ceased to breathe. The smile, remaining, wreathed her countenance to the last. She had gone to her heavenly home!

About grandfather's and grandmother's relatives I know very little,—nothing perhaps of grandma's, and even her own personal knowledge of her kindred was actually quite limited. Grandfather's birthplace and early home was in Malden, Mass. He often spoke of the beauty of that place, and alluded enthusiastically to "Malden's lovely pond."

From a brief account of our family, written in 1870 by a dear sister, whose death occurred in 1888, I learn that grandfather married his first wife, Sarah Pratt, Nov. 17, 1791; removed from Reading, Mass., to Amherst, N. H., in 1792; and there purchased, from Mr. John Damon, the farm which has since continued in our family ownership. The deed was dated Nov. 13, 1792; and the amount paid for the farm was seventy pounds and eighteen shillings. That was our father's birthplace. The house was small, and was built before grandpa bought the place. It was a narrow house, but somewhat longer than now, and opened upon the road on the north side, instead of the south, as it now does. The road then was between the house and barn. When the house was enlarged and remodeled, it extended twelve or fourteen feet farther north than before, and a carriage way was opened on its south side. So where the garden was cultivated during our childhood, adjoining our home on the north, was once the highway.

When the barn was built, or by whom, I cannot say; but I know that now it is in much better condition than at the beginning of my memory of it, sixty-five years ago; and a long annex was added after the farm passed to our brother Jacob's possession.

I remember well, in my childhood, when the ell of the house was built, and the time when all the chambers were unfinished. I then listened to the pattering of the rain upon the roof, and sometimes counted the rafters while lying in bed, having wakened early in the bright summer mornings. But all that has gone by! And the "sweet-apple tree in the corner" is no longer there, nor the broad chestnut on the hillside, nor the spreading cherry tree where the troop of little ones delighted to clamber and frolic. They are gone! So are all the dear faces that once shone joyously about the place: yet the house remains, the home of the fifth Jacob Upham and other loved ones. The old family homestead! It is still in good preservation, well cared for, pleasant, commodious, comfortable, and charmingly retired!

Grandpa had distant relatives in Amherst; but, like himself, they were aged and feeble. I remember several of them being at our father's, but not much concerning them.

Of our father's own mother I have heard but little. I think she was always a feeble woman, a sympathizing friend, and a sincere Christian. Several of her nephews and nieces I re-

member. They all lived in or near Temple and Mason, N. H.
Three of her nieces married, one a Buss, another a Keyes, another a Kendall. One of the daughters of the Buss family, our
second cousin, became our brother George's wife.

Before purchasing his farm in Amherst, grandfather looked
at one in Nashua, on the direct road leading to Boston, which
would not have cost him any more than the one he selected.
But he preferred the one he bought, because it had a much
better orchard and more wood, and was better fitted for cultivation. At another time he was importuned by a gentleman
of Nashua to exchange a handsome and young black horse for
a considerable tract of land there, which has since become
covered with pleasant streets, noble buildings, and fertile
gardens, but it was then a dry, unproductive, dreary waste.
Little did grandpa suppose that a busy manufacturing city
would rise and thrive on that very spot during his lifetime,
drawing into its vortex of varied industries much of the
wealth and business of the pleasant and prospering town in
which he settled. Such was the case. Change is written everywhere!

There was a time when grandfather was not fully satisfied
with his farm. He knew of one in Vermont which he thought
he would prefer to his own. He talked with the owner and
made an even exchange of places. Each farmer removed his
stock, tools, household furniture, and family, to the other
farm, and occupied and worked the new farm a year. The two
men met, and each learned that the other was dissatisfied with
the bargain. So they agreed each to move back to their former home, glad again to possess the one earlier chosen!

Grandfather's mother's maiden name was Rebecca Burnap.
I remember hearing him say that she was a very handsome
woman, and that it was her beauty which first attracted the
attention of his father. He said that on a military parade
day his father was riding horseback and passed Miss Burnap
on the street. She was a stranger to him, but, owing to her
peculiar winning look and manner, he resolved to become acquainted. By some artifice or strategy he managed to pass
her again; and, as he did so, he dropped his whip as if by ac-

cident. She picked it up and handed it to him. Thus commenced the courtship of his parents.

His father died before he was ten years old. His sister
Tammie was sick and died in North Reading, Mass., at the
home of our mother's sister, whose husband, William Tarbox,
was a cousin of our father. It was there, at his aunt's funeral,
that our father and mother first met. The two rode together
when going to the grave. Their acquaintance so commenced
led to their partnership through life.

M.

OUR FATHER AND MOTHER AND THEIR FAMILY.

"To make a happy fireside clime,
To weans and wife—
That's the true pathos and sublime
Of human life."

FATHER.

Almost a century ago, in a sparsely inhabited township in the southern part of New Hampshire, a boy baby gladdened the hearts of a rural couple. He lived, thrived, and grew to manhood amid Nature's manifold diversities. He was born Oct. 29th, 1798. At that time high schools and academies were not as plentiful as now; but the people valued an education and supported district schools. Amherst was an old town and had flourished many years before our father's boyish feet wended their way to the school of the "Cricket Corner district." The first settlers were principally from Massachusetts and brought with them much of her spirit, the spirit, manners, energy, and aspirations of the "Pilgrim Fathers." In that part of the town were many young people. The families I remember, the fathers, mothers, uncles, aunts and cousins, of my youthful associates.

Some of my father's school-books were in the house when I was young. I vividly recollect some of the scenes represented in his spelling-book. The pictures were woodcuts. The arts of illustration have improved greatly since then, and board covers long ago went out of use. His arithmetic was well learned, as shown by his carefully written computations, and gave sufficient knowledge for all common business; and the

geography, for that time, was a good one. Writing was then
done with a goose quill, the letters being formed with exact-
ness and the lines of beauty finely drawn.

In his youth, father, with others of his school companions,
was much given to " trying his strength," performing many
feats of agility, and some wonderful achievements that would
have better been left alone, for he thereby received injuries
from which he never fully recovered. He enjoyed gunning,
trapping, fishing and archery,—a boy among boys.

When older he did not wholly relinquish an indulgence of
pastimes. In the season for wild pigeons he would build a
"pigeon stand " of trimmed trees and poles, enclosing a " bed
place" where corn and buckwheat were laid as bait for the
unsuspecting birds. While they were eating, lo, in an instant
they were captured by a large net sprung over them, the
springing of the net being by means of a rope that extended
to a booth a short distance away, constructed of white pine
boughs, as the pigeoner's hiding place. One year our father
and a neighbor joined in company as pigeoners. They at one
"haul" caught over twenty dozen. Usually ten or twelve dozen
were considered a "good catch." The business was not very
remunerative, and it grew less so, the pigeons becoming more
scarce; but to as late date as 1870 our brothers continued to
catch pigeons in this way nearly every year.

Fox hunting also was a delight to my father; and even after
the growth of my oldest brother he would engage with him in
hunting, trapping, and snaring partridges and rabbits.

He was a militia-man, having, previous to my remembrance
joined the militia company of his native town. The training
and musters were exciting times. He then "camped out," and
returned weary and fagged. When he was in military uni-
form we children had to look up to see our father. A red cap
that he sometimes wore on these occasions reached eight or ten
inches above his head; and his tall, stiff, black leather hat,
embellished with various designs in brasswork, with a long
plume, reached up at least twenty inches beyond the top of
his head. Oh, what a tall man ! The brass buttons on his coat
were rubbed until they glistened like gold; and he always carried a rifle, which likewise must be thoroughly cleaned and
polished before any season of service. With knapsack, can-

teen, and needful ammunition, he went forth to duty, a soldier fitting for his country's need.

During those days one of the militia-men belonging in Amherst was shot by accident or design,—which, was not certain, by whom, not known. A dissipated young man, named Mace, declared that he saw my father do it. The case was tried in court, before a jury. The state procured counsel for father, who lay on the bed, prostrated by the arrogant audacity of his accuser. No one, excepting that notorious knave, would say aught against father; but all who knew him testified of his upright, straightforward, and unswervingly honorable character. He was acquitted. Many thought that the accuser was the murderer, but it was never proved against him.

Father and mother were married November 20th, 1822, several years before the attempt to defame and besmirch his reputation. At no time did my mother's faith in his innocence waver. She was like a blessed angel, giving him courage and support amid heavy affliction. She knew in whom she had placed confidence, and could trust in his goodness even in the darkest hour.

Father was never as well and strong as many men. He had numerous terms of illness, some long, and others shorter. All the while mother, by careful prudence and continual care, looked after the many needs of the house, barn, and farm. Each little one was assigned to some useful employment, increasing the comfort and happiness of the family. She had herself been taught that idleness was a sin, and guarded well against it. Thanks, many and sincere, for such discipline!

Besides working on the farm, father often worked at his trade, which was coopering. He used to carry his manufactured wares, barrels, casks, piggins, kegs, boxes, measures, and whip-stocks, to Salem, Mass., and to Boston, for sale. After his acquaintance with mother, he invariably returned by way of her early home in North Reading. I can remember his going once to sell a load of small kegs, holding from two quarts to four gallons each. The shop had seemed filled to its fullest capacity; and oh, the load, what a big one!

While I was still young, father left the shop mostly for work in the woods; and from that time until his last sickness, he dealt much in wood and lumber, reaping good returns.

When able to work, he was very busy; but could not accomplish as much manual labor as some others whose strength was greater. It was by good calculation, and by a wise improvement of opportunities, that he secured a competence for mother's long widowhood.

Wealth was always aloof from our family; but, as the stewards of God-given time, opportunities and means, father and mother each acknowledged their responsibility, and gave generously according to circumstances. Perhaps no other one in the neighborhood did so much for others in cases of sickness as mother; and father was frequently called on to watch with the sick and dying, always complying if possible.

He was a man of sterling merit. Yet he was not one to command the notice and admiration of strangers; for he was not particularly affable, or prepossessing in manner, but he was thoroughly honest. His word could be depended upon. What he promised to do he did. There were no crafty points in a bargain of his making. Truth and right were his platform. Consequently he stood firmly, conforming his daily life to the divine precept, "All things whatsoever ye would that men should do to you, do ye even so to them."

MOTHER.

Our mother's maiden name was Sarah Hayward. Her birth was August 31st, 1804. She had six brothers and two sisters, two brothers being younger than herself, while all the others were older. Her father, William Hayward, was born, received his education, reared his family, and died, in North Reading, Mass. Her mother's maiden name was Dorcas Townsend, of Lynnfield, Mass.

When I was two or three years old, I visited, with my parents at my mother's former home. Mother then had three little ones to look after. Not long after the arrival, almost as soon as my outside wraps were removed, mother said that I went to the brick oven, pulled down the door, and, still holding it in my hand, swung it around against my back, soiling my dress completely.

I can remember seeing grandma Hayward only twice. The first time was at my father's, within a few years after grandpa Hayward died. She sat beside the blazing fire of our large,

open fire-place; and I still can see, in memory, her black dress,
with the sleeves much wider and looser at the wrists than they
are now made. Again, when I was nine or ten years old, I
well recollect a visit at her home, and the corner closet in the
west front room. Grandma at that time was much bowed over
and to my childish mind seemed very old. The two front
rooms of the house, and the chambers over them, also the
stairs that led to the chambers, and a tree standing near the
house, are indelibly pictured in my mind. What would dear
grandma have thought, could she have looked forward and
seen the new houses of our cousins, Henry and Martin Hayward, and their surroundings, within speaking distance from
the old home?

I have seen the place where my mother went to school, not
the same building, but another on the same site. Mother, I
think, said she had the same teacher nine terms in succession.
In warm weather the scholars were allowed, when good and
studious, to sit on a stone-wall a few feet from the north side
of the school house. Four years ago the wall was still there,
in good condition. Mother told me she had learned many a
lesson sitting there, in the cool shade, fanned by gentle breezes.
One term at a private school of high grade closed her study,
—but not her education, for that was progressing during many
years.

Grandfather Hayward was a singer and belonged to the
church choir; but mother did not understand either vocal or
instrumental music. She greatly enjoyed good singing, and
often said it was a very important and interesting part of the
Sabbath worship. She expressed a wish to unite her voice
with others in praise and thanksgiving. Doubtless she now
joins in heart and voice with the heavenly choir.

She was married when only a little over eighteen years of
age. Previously she had helped her mother spin and weave
towels, table-cloths, and other linen for her future use; and,
with her mother's help, had made the quilts needed for two or
three beds. Her education, acquired in school and at home,
was quite good. Few surpassed her in general knowledge, or
could detect any grammatical errors in her writing or conversation. Her knowledge of housework, sewing, knitting, and
embroidery, was superior to most at the time of her graduation from school.

Shoe-making was then carried on quite extensively, and differently from the present methods in large factories. Nearly every house in her native town had its little shop where men made shoes, the process being finished by the women, who bound them. So, as a matter of course, my mother, before her marriage, did such work. Though young, she became a good wife and mother. Nine of us children were trained to usefulness beneath her care, supplemented by that of our father.

Mother was quite different from father in her general "make-up." She was far more ambitious,—not chiefly for honor, or wealth, though to these she would not object; but, above all else, to excel in virtue and true nobility, in dignity, usefulness, and kindness. She preferred to outdo others in all kinds of nice work, as drawing, painting, and embroidery, rather than to fall below in commonplace. Consequently, during my girlhood, I saw much of her handiwork, done before the many cares of the growing family prevented.

She had much love for the beautiful, both in nature and art. To my youngest sister was transmitted a special taste for drawing and painting, which to a considerable extent she improved. Lizzie greatly enjoyed such work, and left various pieces that we highly prize.

Pictures were a special delight to mother. She long ago said to me, " When young I never wearied of studying a handsome picture; but I am now satisfied,—I have seen enough! " In that way, it seems, God was preparing her for the blindness that followed.

She was constant in attending divine worship, keeping the Sabbath holy. Father and mother united their efforts and influence for the good of their children. Each did well their part, and by example and practice taught the gospel precepts. As soon as their little ones could go to church, they placed them in the Sabbath School. I can now recall words addressed to the school by its superintendent at the time I was in the infant class. That was long ago, in the old church, which had square pews, a pulpit with doors, and a sounding-board over the minister's head.

Two of our mother's brothers were by trade masons; and many were the brick and stone structures they built in Salem, Mass., where they lived. They worked in company, and were ranked among the best masons in New England. One of them, our uncle Josiah, was an earnest abolitionist in the early years of the anti-slavery agitation, when it was unpopular to befriend slaves. But this my uncle did, at the risk of his life and property. The emancipation proclamation by Lincoln was to him a matter of great rejoicing and profound thankfulness.

Our mother outlived all her brothers and sisters. Many families of their children are now living, most, if not all, being within a radius of sixty miles from the old homestead of our maternal grandparents.

Unlike many old persons of her day, mother did not believe it beneficial to use any alcoholic liquors. I remember her saying that the only use she had for rum or alcohol was to dissolve camphor gum. Medicines she preferred to let alone, unless really quite sick. She then consulted a reliable physician, and followed his advice.

Mother lived to the age of eighty-six years, six months, and seventeen days; beloved by her children, grandchildren, and great-grandchildren. She had been entirely blind nine years. During that time she continued to have a lively interest in current events, and, by hearing the general news read and commented upon, she was able, up to her last brief illness, to converse intelligently upon most topics, in an entertaining and interesting manner. She received many friends and callers with evident pleasure and gratification.

Very few have as retentive a memory as our mother. She could with ease and delight repeat more of the Bible and favorite hymns than any other person whom I ever knew. Her enjoyment of life and thankfulness of heart, even while blind, were surprising. She would often count and recount her blessings and mercies, exclaiming in the words of David, "The lines are fallen unto me in pleasant places; yea, I have a goodly heritage."

Less than a year before mother's death, she fell and broke one arm at the wrist. It knit together well, without causing great suffering. But a sudden attack of *la grippe* (influenza), followed by pneumonia, was more than her enfeebled vitality could withstand. She sank rapidly, yet cheerfully, having a well grounded hope of eternal life. On the seventeenth of

March. 1891. death released her submissive spirit from all earthly things. She was done with mortality! Her eyes. so long sightless here. opened to the rapturous vision of a redeemed saint. purified. immortal. glorified.

JACOB.

Our oldest brother was our mother's first born and most tenderly loved child. He was a pretty boy. with dark hazel eyes and very dark brown hair that naturally parted in the middle. which annoyed him as he grew older. He sometimes would tease my sister Sarah and myself. disturb us while quietly at play. throw down our little play-houses, and then tell us that we ought to have made them stronger: yet he was kind and affectionate. and. in his manhood. sought and improved many opportunities of kindness and charity to unfortunate, needy, and sorrowing ones.

I loved this brother dearly. When a young man he went to Pennsylvania to help construct one of the many railroads then being built. He was absent from home a long time. His return was unexpected. The family were eating their evening meal. The school teacher had accompanied a younger brother home. and witnessed the happy occasion. the great gladness and hilarity of the meeting. He said that the children fairly danced for joy; and the delight of the parents seemed no less. though more quiet.

Often in the summers my husband. Mr. Kelley, spent a few days or weeks with Jacob in pigeoning, for which, and for hunting foxes and other game. he inherited a fondness from our father.

In the winters. brother Jacob for many years engaged in lumbering. buying wood-lots within two or three miles from the Amherst home. cutting them off and selling the wood and lumber at a good profit. Here, too. he gained much through the experience and ability acquired in his association with our father in his earlier similar enterprises.

During some other and later winters brother Jacob, and afterward George, sold garden seeds for A. H. Dunlap & Sons, of Nashua. driving one to two months or more in a single absence from home. on routes through New Hampshire, Vermont. Massachusetts, Rhode Island, Connecticut, and New York.

In the year 1871 my brother Jacob married, and two little
ones, a daughter and a son, cheered the loving hearts of the
parents: but when the youngest was only a few months old,
the mother died, and at the age of a little more than a year
the baby followed her. My grief-stricken brother, knowing
that the little daughter needed mother-love and care, married
again, and another son took his father's name. He now is a
young man, and, with his mother, has the charge of the old
Upham homestead farm.

Five years ago our brother Jacob died, apparently without
a minute's warning, near the end of a day in early winter.
He had seemed in his usual health, and had just reached home
from a journey to Nashua with his horse and wagon. The
cause of his death was heart failure, but it was wholly unexpected by himself or his family. He survived our dear mother
only a few months. We were thankful that God spared him
until she left us: it would have been so hard for her to bear
the sorrow of parting.

SARAH.

Our grandfather Upham's sister Tamzan, in her last illness,
gave to him a string of gold beads which she had herself
worn, and told him to keep them until my father married:
then to give them to him, with the injunction that his first
daughter should be named Tamzan and be the owner of the
beads. Mother's second child was a daughter, and to the little wee baby they gave the name Tamzan, and the gold beads!
Mother's name was Sarah, and the name of each of my grandfather's two wives was Sarah. So it was determined that that
name should precede Tamzan. My sister was always called
Sarah. She wore the beads many years. They were of medium size, and unusually smooth and handsome.

But the time came when gold beads were considered out of
fashion, and were rarely worn by girls. In her earnest Christian devotion Sarah felt a longing desire to sell them and de-
vote the proceeds to the missionary cause. She told mother
of her wish and intention, and mother bought the beads; giving her, I think, eight dollars, which sum she gladly contributed to foreign missions. I do not think my sister ever
regretted having parted with the beads: for till her death,

when thirty-four years old, she was always ready to make
sacrifices that she might help spread abroad righteousness,
holiness, and true happiness. Evidently her main purpose and
desire was the accomplishment of good : this was indicated by
her general character, her manner of life from day to day.

Sister Sarah appreciated good books and good company.
She was a Bible student, and was the teacher of a class of
young ladies in the Sabbath School.

Her health was precarious for several years. From girlhood
she was inclined to cough. While her husband made shoes,
she kept a little store as a milliner and fancy goods dealer, at
their home in Salem village, and to buy her goods went frequently to Boston. Two years, or more, before her death she
realized that her lungs were far from well. Talking with me,
she said, "I think I may die suddenly from hemorrhage of
the lungs. If this should happen when I am away from home,
tell father and mother that I wish them to take my two little
girls, and God will reward them."

The time of her departure was not then. She outlived
father more than a year, and at last was confined to her bed
for weeks. Meanwhile the Saviour was her portion, confidence, and hope. He was leading her.

> " Breezes of balm blow from those shores immortal,
>   Soft sleep the billows in the radiance fair ;
>   Angelic forms, beside each heavenly portal,
>   Wait to receive and bid us welcome there."

MARY.

Of my mother's children I was the third. Grandpa Upham
wished me called Mary for a sister of his. I now have silver
sleeve-buttons which in those long ago years belonged to that
sister.

I commenced going to school very young, but during the
first term I did not enjoy it. Being bashful, I did not like to
leave my seat to read. The teacher compelled me to go to
her desk, but that sometimes was almost more than she could
do! The same teacher was applied to for the next term, but
refused, because, as she said, it was too trying to her patience
to get along with me, a little, wee bit of a girl, four years and
six months old! Other teachers had no trouble.

When I was ten years old that same lady was again employed as teacher. She acknowledged that no one in school at that time was more lovable, dutiful, or obedient than I. To study was my delight, and, on my reaching the age of sixteen, the superintendent of schools told my father that, if I wished, he would give me a certificate for teaching any common school. But I was often on the bed with severe headache, and for that reason chose other employment.

I went to service in families, assisting in general housework. I also worked awhile in "the mills" at Nashua (as cotton factories were usually designated), but only a little, because my health was insufficient for the task. When at home I assisted mother.

On the evening of Thanksgiving Day, in 1847, I was married, being that day twenty years and eight months old. Four of my children still live, all being situated near me in Salem, N. H.; and my younger daughter, who is a widow, with her two boys, lives with me. This town was also their father's native place and continuous home. Arthur, seventeen years of age, is the oldest of my grandchildren.

I was the first to marry in my father's family, and have been a widow twelve years. Well do I know the deep, unutterable loneliness of widowhood; when the long-loved, affectionate, and sympathizing companion and friend is gone, never to return, and responsibilities unknown before press heavily. Of what exceeding worth are now the consolations of the gospel of Christ, the Saviour of the world! How sweet to know that the everlasting God is my guardian and my guide!

The death of sister Lizzie, who had very tenderly and affectionately cared for our mother, brought the necessity that some other one should fill that responsible position. After much deliberation, it was determined that I should assume this duty; and for nearly three years I endeavored to perform it to the best of my ability, remaining with mother, attending to her needs, and attentively considering her comfort and pleasure, until she went to our Heavenly Father. In his arms she needs nothing; "there are pleasures forevermore." Since then, in earning the needed livelihood for myself and others, nursing the sick has occupied a considerable portion of my time.

Through the varied scenes of my life God has ever been with me. Once a terrible illness carried me very near the grave,—so that the clothes for my burial were in readiness. But to the kindness of a skillful physician, with the unremitting care of dear friends, and above all to the blessing of the great Health-Giver, I owe my continued lease of life for yet a while longer, and my clear memory well stored with recollections of the past. Some of these remembrances I wish to have told to generations following, that they may know somewhat of the history of the family and be able to form intelligent and correct ideas of their ancestry.

EMILY.

My mother's fourth child was Emily Dorcas, the second name being for grandmother Hayward. She was more emotional in her nature than many; more sensitive, perhaps, than any other one of our family. Her social feelings were strong. She had ardent affection for each member of the family. When living at a distance from the others, as was the case during all her married life, she would always meet us with intense pleasure. I especially recollect mother's speaking of a visit to her at one time. She said that Emily saw her, and those with her, approaching, and ran with open arms to the door, ready for a warm and affectionate embrace.

Very different were the emotions of meeting and of parting. Leave-taking generally brought tears! Yet her relations to each husband were remarkably felicitous: she fully enjoyed her family and housekeeping.

She had great powers for conversation and could entertain and keep a roomful of company in laughter the whole evening, without being nonsensical. She was frank, open-hearted, and generous, possibly too much so! She was greatly moved to pity, desirous to amend all the sorrow she came in contact with. Her sympathy often abated grief and alleviated trouble. She was a friend to the friendless, a helper to lift the fallen and unfortunate. Her favorite present for her younger sisters and brothers was the Bible.

Sister Emily was married twice, and left a daughter by each husband. Her last sickness was short; a severe fever raged about two weeks. Her husband told me, after her death, that

during the first few days of her illness she was very desirous
for him to remain by her constantly, yet he thought he could
not leave his work ; but when her mind, in the fever delirium,
wandered, recognizing him only at intervals, he had no heart
to leave her.

SUSAN.

This sister is now the only one I have to love and visit, the
others having passed beyond the toil and perplexities of the
present life. Susan was considerably younger than I, and
consequently my school days were mostly passed before hers
began.

At the age of about sixteen years she was employed as
teacher in her home district. I recall hearing her speak of
taking special pains with one boy who was remarkably dull.
She said that, with all her strenuous efforts, she did not succeed in advancing him very much. Yet when he grew up,
there was not any noticeable inferiority of intellect.

Susan was skillful with a needle, and at one time applied
herself to binding shoes, boarding in the family of a friend.
By close application she averaged to lay up about seventy-
five cents a day besides paying for board.

One summer Susan spent several weeks with me on the farm
which was my first home in Salem. There was a beautiful
pond (then called Policy pond, but now Canobie lake), not
far distant, where she enjoyed angling. A friend called to
see her one day and they went fishing together. The next day
it so happened that I went into her chamber, and there hung
a pair of wet laced boots. Upon inquiry she told me that she
was standing on a rock which projected into the water, and
that, when rather excited on account of catching more fish
than usual, she threw her line farther than she intended and
lost her balance. Her friend, close by, pulled her out of the
water, and she hastened to the house and changed all her ap-
parel, without any suspicions on my part that she had been in
danger! She often went fishing afterward; but never again
jumped into the pond!

When she was at my home, Rev. John N. Chase, of Exeter,
N. H., then a boy of fifteen, came to help about the farm
work. Susan said, "I have met his mother, and I think the

son of such a mother will do well." He did; and when he left us, it was like parting with a brother.

Not often are two sisters more interested each for the other than Susan and I. The cord that binds us may be broken for this world; but shall we not live on, on, and love eternally? And will not the Lord between us watch over each of us through this earthly life, "when we are absent one from another?"

JOHN.

The birth of a second son in the family was a matter of rejoicing, after four daughters. This brother, John Henry by name, met with a very serious and painful accident while at work, soon after his marriage, cutting with an ax into the knee-joint. That laid him on the bed and kept him there several weeks. Rather a dark honey-moon!

His knee has never been very well or strong since, yet sufficiently so to permit walking and work with little or no inconvenience. Within the past year, however, it has been again the occasion of much pain and discomfort, and it still continues very weak and lame.

In the spring of 1868, six years after his marriage, brother John narrowly escaped from being drowned. His horse, harnessed in the wagon, became frightened and jumped off the ferry-boat, crossing the Merrimack river at Thornton's Ferry. John had endeavored to check the horse, but at last was obliged to jump for his life into the river, rather than be struck by the wagon as it went overboard. Encumbered by his overcoat and rubber boots, he swam in the very cold water several rods to the shore.

When young, brother John had an inclination for writing poetry, much of which appeared in the newspapers of that time. It was a fancy of his youth, wholly neglected in after years.

One Sabbath, when a little fellow, three or four years old, he stayed with me while the others of the family went to church. He was resolute and naughty, and determined not to do what I wished. I told him that unless he would, I would shut him in the cellar. "Well," he said, "then I will go to the milk-closet, and tip over all the pans of milk." I felt that he was not to be trusted, and therefore, of course, not to be disgraced by being put in the cellar.

I wonder whether he remembers going from post to post along the fence surrounding the grave-yard near the schoolhouse, hunting for birds' nests. The posts alternated in height, one tall and the next short; and usually we would find a redbreast robin's nest on every short post. To the credit of the schoolboys, be it said, the nests were very seldom disturbed, although they were looked at every day.

Brother John is an expert trapper, and in his youth and early manhood he accumulated considerable money by that means, and by buying furs, taking them to Boston for sale. In boyhood, like my brothers George and Warren later, he snared many partridges and rabbits each autumn, beginning a savings bank account by the proceeds of their sale when sent to the Faneuil market in Boston.

The home of brother John and Katie, his wife, was formerly that of her parents. It is picturesque and lovely. The house, situated on a low hill, is somewhat quaint, and is sufficiently large for convenience. Closely adjoining it on the west is a grove of tall white pines, only a few rods distant from cultivated vines, shrubs, and a large variety of flowers, blended amid full grown and wide-spreading apple trees. Projecting here and there from the fertile soil are ledges of rock, beside which grow many a fragrant geranium, columbine, peony, and flower-de-luce.

Meandering past is the Souhegan river, its waters gurgling and splashing as they flow amid the rocks and stones, to the little mill-pond, strong dam, and waterfall, at my brother's mill, close by, for sawing lumber and grinding corn. Last year, when I visited there, the sweet-scented summer air needed not to be shut out from my chamber; and the gentle murmurings of the river were a constant lullaby quieting to restful sleep.

Our brother's postal address is Thornton's Ferry, N. H.; but he continues to attend church nearly every Sunday at Amherst, about three and a half miles distant. There during many years he has been, like our ancestor of the same name, the emigrant John Upham, more than two hundred years ago, a deacon of the Congregational church.

LIZZIE.

As this sister grew she exhibited a passion for drawing and painting, and was almost continually making sketches of persons, places, and things. As soon as her schooling was completed, she by study and practice became proficient in various branches of drawing and painting, and made preparation to be a teacher of art, intending to commence her work in Salem, Mass., where her home at first would be with our uncles and cousins. She had packed her trunk for leaving home, when father called her to his room, and requested of her a promise that, instead of going, she would remain and assist in the work and cares which must soon devolve upon our mother. Father was ill, able to sit up but little. He told her that he thought it would be his last sickness—and so it proved—and he wished her to be all a dutiful daughter could be to console and comfort our mother in her grief and sorrow. She made the promise and faithfully kept it. How faithfully and well God knows, and will reward; the joys of an approving conscience were given her in this life,—the joys and glory of heaven will be eternal!

When our father lay dying, sister Lizzie bent her head low that she might catch his last whisper. But, with tears in her eyes, she told me that she could not understand, so inarticulate had become his voice.

She remained on the home farm with mother twelve years. Then Jacob bought the old homestead, and mother bought a house in Nashua (No. 36, Lock street) to which she and sister Lizzie removed. It was their home, and, till my youngest brother had a home of his own, it was his home also, though he was absent the greater part of the time in his work of surveying.

With what care and taste did sister Lizzie arrange every article of furniture, and the many pictures on the walls of each room! How thriftily grew all her plants! The sun's rays seemed more genial there than elsewhere; and the apples, peaches, plums, cherries, and smaller fruits of the garden, were luscious. Yet insidious disease came, pulmonary consumption, by which our father, sister Sarah, her two daughters,

Lizzie and Josie, and our brother George and his wife Sarah, had died; and on a summer day, July 20th, 1888, at the age of nearly fifty years, sister Lizzie was with us no more!

Though she and our mother both died in Nashua, their burial was in Amherst, in the lot which father had bought in the cemetery close to the Cricket Corner schoolhouse, where in our childhood we attended school. There have all the deceased of the family been carried, except brother Jacob, who chose a lot for himself and family in the new cemetery of Amherst village.

Sister Lizzie's baptismal name was Ruth Elizabeth. Grandfather Upham wished her called Ruth, in memory of his youngest sister, whose death was about thirty years before my sister's birth. When she was small we often used both names; but as she grew older she objected, wishing only the appellation "Lizzie," and by that name alone she was known to many.

She had a strong desire to outlive mother, as she feared no one else could so tenderly care for her. But God otherwise ordered. She submitted, at first sorrowfully, but at last trustfully, saying, "Our Heavenly Father will do all right."

After her death, my brothers, sisters, and myself, asked each other, "Who will take care of mother?" I accepted the responsibility, regretting that dear sister Lizzie could not, previous to her departure, have known the plans for mother's comfort through the remainder of her life, nearly three years, continuing in her Nashua home.

Lizzie never married, because she might then be less able to give her whole life to the comfort and happiness of others, and especially of mother. She had a smile for everybody. Her quiet and unobtrusive manner won for her many friends and greatly increased the power of her influence.

She was an efficient Sabbath School teacher, both at Amherst and Nashua, taking a real interest for the souls and for the bodily welfare of those entrusted to her care. None were so mean and unworthy that she would not seek to uplift and help them. So broad were her sympathies that she wished, as far as practicable, yes, as far as possible, to benefit all. The instruction given to her pupils, who, through many years, growing from childhood to womanhood, remained under her

teaching, will forever endure, being taught and inculcated by
mothers to their children, and affecting all following generations. The hymns at her funeral were sung by members of
her former class of the Sabbath School of the First Congregational church at Nashua.

JESSE.

One son, Jesse Hayward Upham, named for a brother and a
nephew of our mother, was born February 10, 1841, and died
March 3, 1841. The physician said that this baby, so early
transplanted to the heavenly home, was never well. Yet I
think it was about a week after its birth before the baby's
illness became evident to the family.

Two or three weeks after the burial of the little one, sister
Lizzie, then about two and a half years old, was absent a long
time from the room. I went to look for the missing child and
found her standing on a chair looking out of a window. The
snow was fast falling, in large damp flakes. I stood silent
and motionless just inside the door. She turned and as soon
as her eyes met mine burst into tears, saying, "It snows right
on little Jesse's grave," and for some minutes could not be
comforted.

GEORGE.

Among my brothers, George was the merriest and most
witty, but not especially talkative. He would amuse both old
and young with the drolleries which he would comically re-
late, though using only a few words. His pleasant and winning ways made him a favorite with us all.

He was a true Christian, and endeavored by word and example to win others to a love for holiness of heart and life.
Cheerfulness with him was a matter of principle and purpose.
He said that, if he ever felt sad or discouraged, it was no reason why he should say or do aught to disturb the pleasure of
others. He strenuously tried to be happy himself, and to
make others happy.

My brothers enjoyed the games of checkers, backgammon,
and dominoes; and we all found pleasure in solving riddles,
charades, and enigmas. George outdid most others in solving
these puzzles.

In his boyhood George, and later Warren, as soon as each was ten years old, went to market in Nashua every week in summer and autumn, or two or three times weekly when the wild blueberries, huckleberries, and blackberries were ripening abundantly, to sell these berries picked by our mother, brothers, and sisters, and to sell the peas, beans, sweet corn, potatoes, turnips, squashes and melons, currants, cherries, apples, butter, eggs, chickens, and other products of the farm. Rising early and starting to market usually before sunrise, with the family horse and wagon, they drove the distance of ten miles to the city, spent two or three hours in calling from house to house, selling their load, and then returned in season usually for dinner at home and the afternoon's work.

George, like our brother John, was very successful in trapping, and in buying and selling furs. He had much mechanical and inventive skill, shown in boyhood by ingeniously whittled toys, and later by using improved farming implements, as the mowing-machine and horse-rake, and keeping them in repair.

During the winters of his later years, George was a traveling salesman for A. H. Dunlap, dealer in garden seeds, of Nashua. In his last winter, though weakened by disease, he kept at work with unremitting perseverance. He said he would not live long if he should give up labor. He grew more and more feeble, yet continued until near the middle of the winter, when he felt that he could no longer do justice to his employer. He left his team at Pittsfield, Mass., and looked for the last time on the beautiful hill and mountain scenery which he had come to love during many times of travel over that route; took the cars, and got home as quickly as possible; and within a few weeks he died.

His feebleness, while still traveling with his team, had called forth the sympathy of others. My brother, when speaking of it, said, " I had been on the route so long that all knew me, and they were exceedingly kind in doing all lifting and other waiting on me with evident pleasure; else I would have been obliged to quit much sooner."

He was solicitous for his two boys, who, he knew, would soon be motherless; but when told by a sister-in-law, brother Jacob's wife, Sarah, that she would do for them as for her

own, he sank back upon his pillow, saying, " How much eas-
ier, now, it will be to die."

WARREN.

This youngest one of our family was the most fond of books,
and learned to read quite well at the age of three years. He
attended the district school, and afterward was in the academy at Mont Vernon, N. H., and in the Amherst high school,
each for one term. At the age of seventeen he entered Dart-
mouth College, in Hanover, N. H., and took the classical
course, graduating in 1871. Meantime he earned, by working several hours a day, and teaching school between the college terms, nearly enough to meet all his expenses.

After his graduation he engaged in civil engineering for
the system of water works in Concord, N. H., and for railroad
surveys in the region of the White mountains. Later he was
assistant on the geological survey of New Hampshire, with
Prof. C. H. Hitchcock, the state geologist; and later still he
was assistant on the Minnesota Geological Survey, with Prof.
N. H. Winchell, state geologist. Afterward he was engaged
during seven years, next after his marriage in 1885, for the
United States Geological Survey, and partly for Canada, his
field of exploration and reports being the valley of the Red
river of the North and the basin of lakes Winnipeg and Manitoba, occupied during the closing part of the Ice Age by the
glacial lake Agassiz.

In the spring of 1895 he became librarian for the Western
Reserve Historical Society, in Cleveland, Ohio; but in the
early autumn of the same year he was elected as secretary
and librarian of the Minnesota Historical Society, in St. Paul,
Minn., and began his work there November 1st. This society
has a library of 59,000 volumes, free to the public, in the
State Capitol.

From 1885 to 1893 Warren lived in West Somerville, Mass.
(at No. 36, Newbury street, on Clarendon hill), excepting long
absences in the summers for geological exploration in Minnesota, North Dakota, and Manitoba. His wife Addie during the
later part of that time was a member of the Somerville school
board through a term of three years. She is interested, at
their Minnesota home, in the work of the Woman's Christian

Temperance Union, and of the Plymouth Congregational church and Sunday School, in which they are members. They are much interested in Carleton College, Northfield, Minn., where Addie, before their marriage, had studied three years.

OUR AMHERST HOME LIFE.

Our childhood home will be forever held in affectionate remembrance. Our parents considered the cultivation of the mind and heart as important as that the body receive proper attention. Their teachings were both by example and precept, to be honest, truthful and upright, in all places and under all circumstances.

In the morning the children were expected to be up early and in readiness for the table as soon as the breakfast was ready. When all were seated and quiet, a blessing was sought from the Great Giver of all good, and thanks were rendered for our daily food. After breakfast, before the members of the family dispersed, came the morning prayer by father, seeking for each one strength and guidance for the day's duties. However much business was on hand to be done, it did not push aside the spending of a short time in devotion and prayer. Nor did his prayer displace later unspoken petitions; for we were taught to call on God in silence and to seek his protecting power at all times, and to heartily praise him for blessings and favors. When very young we were taught the great difference there is between heartfelt desire going forth to God, and thoughtless saying of prayers.

When old enough to go to school, we were started off every morning early. Each one received a "good-bye" from mother as they started, dinner-pail in hand, and a firm injunction to be good. On returning from school, most usually came the question, "Have you been good to-day?" Mother's approval was invaluable,—without it came sorrow and heartache!

Besides the habits of industry, whether in studies or in daily tasks of work, that were required, we had portions of every day allotted for play. A most attractive combination of work and play was the care of a flower plat in the garden adjoining the house on the north. As we successively grew, each of us children took great pleasure in preparing the ground, planting our seeds, and tenderly caring for many showily flowering plants, as tulips, peonies, roses, pinks, marigolds, and a multitude of others. Each had his or her little garden plat, where individual diligence and skill were repaid by the beauties of the flowers blooming through all the long summer time.

West of the house is an elm, thriftily growing, which brother John set out about forty years ago. May it see the year 2000!

Such was our home-training that Sunday was of all days the best. The early morning gave time for a last look at the Sunday School lesson, which was heard and explained by the teacher during the intermission between two sermons. After the church service, while riding home, or while eating dinner, each one was questioned more or less about the sermon, and we were expected to be able to find the texts.

We had only two meals on Sunday, the second one coming as soon as practicable after our arrival at home from church. Afterward there was considerable time for reading, and invariably all joined awhile in reading successively one or two verses from the Bible. Sometimes we would read several chapters in that way. Later, at twilight, and before the lighting of lamps, all the family joined in successive recital of hymns and portions of the Bible, especially of the Psalms. Those hours are indelibly fixed in my memory. Seldom passes a Sabbath without my mind reverting pleasurably to them. They are among the happiest recollections of my childhood.

Many a time, when cares have pressed heavily, the thought that my father and mother bore with patience and courage the many trials and perplexities of life, trusting always in God, has given me hope, and added strength to strength, and made more perfect my faith in sustaining grace. What they had endured, could not I? The same good Lord who sustained them is my Father, Friend, and Guide.

The quiet submission, faith, patience, hopefulness, and courage of my parents have ever been an inspiration and help to me. Our early home was truly a Christian home. I remember it with affection and shall ever cherish fond recollections of those early days and that paternal teaching. Thanks to the Great Ruler of all for such a home, for its happy memories, its lasting influence, and for all the dear ones there.

M.

GOOD OLD AMHERST.

"Land where our fathers died,
Land of the pilgrim's pride."

During more than a century the home of our branch of the
Upham family has been in Amherst, near the center of Hillsborough county, N. H., of which it was the shire town or
county seat, until that distinction was usurped by the fast
growing cities of Manchester and Nashua. In its history Amherst is one of the most interesting towns of the Granite State.
At the time of our grandfather's removal thither, it was surpassed in population, and probably in social and political influence, by no more than five towns of New Hampshire, name-
ly, Portsmouth, Rochester, Londonderry, Gilmanton, and Bar-
rington.

The following concise review of the leading events of Amherst history is derived from various histories and gazetteers
of New Hampshire, and especially from Secomb's *History of
the Town of Amherst* (978 pages, 1883) and a historical dis-
course, by Rev. J. G. Davis, on January 19, 1874, the hundredth
anniversary of the dedication of the Congregational meeting-
house.

1728. According to acts passed by the General Court of the province
of Massachusetts Bay, the area now known as Amherst, N. H., was
surveyed and granted to soldiers who had served in the Narraganset
War of 1675-76, and to their heirs. It was at first known as Narraganset No. 3, and later as Souhegan West.

1734. The earliest settlement within the limits of Amherst, by families from northeastern Massachusetts.

1739. The first meeting-house built.

1740. The boundary line between Massachusetts and New Hampshire established as now. The former province till this time claimed a
large area north of that line, including Amherst.

1760. This township, having 110 resident taxpayers, was incorporated under its present name, in honor of Gen. Jeffrey Amherst, then commander-in-chief of the British forces in North America.

1769. New Hampshire was divided into five counties, with Amherst as the shire town of Hillsborough county.

1770. Monson township, which had included the parts of Amherst and Milford south of the Souhegan river, surrendered its charter, and its territory was divided and annexed to Amherst and Hollis.

1771-1774. The second meeting-house was built, still in use by the Congregational church.

1775-1783. Amherst, having in 1775 a population of 1,428, furnished 300 soldiers and sailors to the service of the country, but many of them for only a short time, in the Revolutionary War; and 32 of her soldiers lost their lives in the war.

1794. First and only session of the State Legislature at Amherst. The new township of Milford was incorporated this year, including the former Southwest Parish of Amherst, with adjoining tracts. In 1790, previous to this cession, Amherst had a population of 2,369.

1802. The Farmer's Cabinet, a weekly newspaper, founded by Joseph Cushing; after 1809 conducted by Richard Boylston and his son, Edward D. Boylston; published in Amherst ninety years; now removed to Milford.

1803. Mont Vernon was incorporated, having formerly been the Northwest Parish of Amherst. In 1800 Amherst had a population of 1,470; and Milford, 939. By the census of 1810 the population of the three towns was found to be, in Amherst, 1,554; Milford, 1,117; and Mont Vernon, 762.

1812-1815. War with Great Britain; many soldiers and seamen from Amherst, but the full records remain unpublished.

1848. The Wilton railroad was built from Nashua to Danforth's Corner, now called Amherst station. It was extended to Milford and East Wilton in 1851.

1861-1865. The Civil War; from a population of 1,508 in 1860, Amherst supplied 96 of her men to the army, and six to the navy; and 33 other Amherst men were represented in the army by substitutes. The Soldiers' Monument, bearing the names of the 26 Amherst soldiers who lost their lives in the war, was erected in 1871.

The frontispiece of Secomb's History of this town is a map of its area, showing the location of dwellings, drafted by the present writer. Going southeast from Amherst village on the road crossing Tuck bridge, our old home is reached at the distance of about two miles. It is in the angle of the first branch road leading east.

An unnamed brook, in which the writer swam and fished when a boy, is crossed by this branch road on the east edge of the homestead farm. The next farm, with its house not far from the brook, was successively owned in my boyhood and later by Mr. Josiah W. Pillsbury and our brothers John and George. My chief playmate, Albert E. Pillsbury, has since been, during several sessions, President of the Massachusetts Senate, and later the Attorney General of that state.

Well do I remember where my brother George and I were repairing the stone-walls of the pasture, close north of the house that had been grandfather's, when, in the spring of 1865, Mr. Pillsbury returned from a journey to the village, bringing the sad news of the assassination of Lincoln. Almost five years earlier I attended a presidential campaign rally one evening in Milford, where an illuminated canvas-covered wagon bore the portrait of Lincoln, and the words, "The Man for the Crisis." Little could I understand, or could even the wisest foresee, how terrible that crisis and war must be! Four years earlier, in 1856, among my first remembrances, was a presidential rally in Amherst for Fremont and Dayton, with the raising of a flag on a "liberty pole" about a hundred feet high.

No other views will ever seem to me more beautiful than the outlook northward from the top of the hill descending to Mr. Newton Lowe's, about halfway between our home and the village, as we saw it on Sunday mornings of clear weather in riding or walking to church. Over and far beyond the village of "Amherst Plain," which was in the foreground, from the Uncanoonuck mountains, on the northeast, westward by Joe English hill and Mont Vernon, to the Lyndeborough and Peterborough or Pack Monadnock mountains (the last being sometimes white with snow in late autumn when only rain had fallen elsewhere), was a view that I shall never forget. It was not so grand a prospect, nor was "our brook" so large, as many others seen since; but they then filled a larger part in my life than any scenery and experiences of maturer years.

Many excursions I took, on an "Election Day" (early in June) or the Fourth of July, with boy comrades and my brother George, along the Souhegan river, to spear or slip-noose its pickerel or chubs; to Babboosuck pond, hiring a boat and angling for the delicious horned pouts; to Joe English

hill; and to Purgatory, a deep and picturesque rock gulch on
the west line of Mont Vernon. Among my companions in those
tramps, and afterward in long excursions through the White
mountains and to Connecticut and Umbagog lakes, the one
best known through all the later years is William F. Flint,
the botanist, now of Winchester, N. H.   He lived far from us,
on the Wilkins hill, southwest of the village.

   Our school district was No. 3, or "Cricket Corner." It was
so named, according to an ancient tradition, for its wonderful
multitude, during occasional seasons, of the black, chirping
insects called crickets.   The Pillsbury farm belonged to the
"Pond Parish" district, next northeastward, to which our
home farm was afterward annexed.   There also the Converse
boys, Charles, Luther, and Robert, all still living in Amherst,
brothers of our sister-in-law Sarah, attended school.   In our
Cricket Corner district, my schoolmates included Albert D.
Melendy, now of Nashua; Miles J. Merrill and the late George
E. Holt, also of Nashua; Gustavus G. Fletcher, of Chatta-
nooga, Tenn.; and James F. Weston and his sisters, Clara and
Lizzie, of Amherst.

   Through two or three winter terms, it was my task, at the
age of ten to twelve years, to build the fire each morning in
that schoolhouse, coming earliest of all, a half hour or more
before school time; for which the ashes, worth a dollar or
more, were a full or partial payment.

   On the neighboring "big meadow," when a January thaw
had covered it with water by the rise of the Souhegan river,
followed by severe freezing, we had glorious skating.   In the
beautiful starlit evenings we carried wood and built a large
fire on the ice.   Then Capt. George W. Fletcher, and other
staid old citizens, would renew their youth, buckle on their
skates, and show us boys how to "cut the figure 8."

   In the spelling-class it was customary for the teacher to
offer a prize for the one that would be at the head of the class
the most days of the term, in which Addie Holt, who died long
ago, was my principal competitor.   The earliest teacher whom
I fully remember, and who often chastised me as I deserved
and now am thankful for, was Maria Caldwell, now Mrs.
George Hill of Merrimack.   Later teachers, whom I affectionately remember, were L. Augusta Bruce of Mont Vernon,

Martha Wilder of Peterborough, and Vrylena L. Shattuck of
Jaffrey. After reaching the age of seven years, it was my
highest happiness at school to please the teacher by good be-
havior as much as by making good progress in studies.

The same schoolhouse remains. It was built, I think, about
a hundred years ago. In the same place, and probably in the
same schoolhouse, our father received his education; and, in
the later years, all our brothers and sisters. The last time
when I went inside it my brother Jacob and I, one June day
of 1890, spent an hour or more in listening to the recitations
of children whose parents, in some instances, had been our
schoolmates.

Close south of the schoolhouse is the cemetery where most
of our deceased Amherst kindred are buried. There, in every
visit to good old Amherst, and as I stroll over the pastured
hills of our old farm, my mind is filled with countless tender
memories of our father and mother, Lizzie, George, and all the
dear ones who have preceded us and bade us farewell, until
that happy day when our father's and mother's prayers shall
be answered in our being all reunited in heaven.

W.

SELECTIONS FROM WRITINGS
OF MARY UPHAM KELLEY.

Some of these writings have been published in newspapers, and as regular contributions, during several years, in a magazine in Boston, devoted to local and special charities. Many others remain unpublished. They all are short, being sketches of events, persons, places, or things: thoughts of cheer, aspiration, or Christian devotion; and precepts, teaching, or entertainment, for the young. They were written in minutes and half hours of leisure and rest, amid heavy household cares and toil for the home and its loved ones. Packages of these writings are a part of the gifts bequeathed, with a mother's love, to my children and grandchildren.

THE ANCIENT BUREAU.
Written in November, 1889.

This bureau used to stand in my mother's parlor in Amherst when I was a little girl, but in Nashua it has stood in her sleeping apartment many years. It is of mahogany, so cut and put together that the lines of yearly growth of the wood meet centrally on each drawer, forming a lovely figure. The brass knobs are not so lustrous as once, but they might easily be polished and thus regain their primitive beauty.

In that bureau were deposited for safe keeping the large copper cents given to me, and to my brothers and sisters, by teamsters who stopped at our well to drink. In those far away times loaded wagons often passed our house, carrying flour, molasses, and other commodities and merchandise, drawn by two, four, or six horses, from Nashua, and sometimes even from Boston, to the pretty, thriving village of Amherst, which was then the seat of trade for towns farther back in the country. My father lived on the "county road," and it was much travelled during many years, before the building of the Wilton railroad.

Grand old bureau! Sixty and seven years have come and gone since the wedding clothes of my parents were carefully folded and laid in those drawers, that no dust should soil them. Since then what numberless garments for old and young have been hidden in its recesses! How many little baby-gowns have been taken from those hiding places. —no chest or trunk so convenient! And there always could be found mother's best pillow-cases, so nice that they were seldom used.

There are two little drawers above the others, and over these a long, narrow strip of mahogany with carving and brass ornamentations. On the top of the little drawers, when I was young, always sat two very small trunks,—one a present to my mother from her brother Aaron, his own handwork, in which she kept little trinkets not in everyday use. In the other, which I never ceased to admire, my father kept writings.

How pleasant the memory of those times, when on Sunday morning the drawers were opened, and, if in summer, little round white capes, arm-mitts, ruffled pantalets, white stockings, and ankle-tie shoes, or prunella slippers, were found and brought from their snug quarters by my mother and placed upon her four little girls, of which I was the second in age.

Mother never forgot, too, the clean handkerchiefs. My brother's was put in his pocket, but we girls had no pockets; consequently the handkerchief was pinned to the belt of the dress just a little in front of the right arm. Father carried a yellow bandanna with white polka-spots. These all were kept in that notably useful bureau.

WILLIE ASTRAY.

It was a delightful Sabbath in the later part of summer, a very beautiful day. There was no cloud to obscure the ethereal blue, nor wind to shake the thick foliage of green. The balmy air was melodious with the hum of insects, the chirping of crickets, and the songs of many happy birds. Wild flowers were abundant, and the orchards were loaded with luscious fruit. All nature seemed rejoicing in the goodness and wisdom of the infinite Creator.

A large, handsome, old-fashioned farm-house, on the road from Salem Depot to Methuen, was the home of a little boy left alone on that day with his mamma. He had a brother and sisters, but they had gone with his papa to church. Willie, as the little boy was named, had the freedom of the spacious grounds, and of a long hall running through the house from side to side. The mother, as was her habit, improved much of the time in reading; while the little one, the pet of the family, played with the demure old puss, or waggishly pulled the long hair of Lion, the family dog, looking up often for mamma's smile of commendation, or to listen to some story she had to tell.

Occasionally Willie would go out of doors onto the lawn, to watch the scattered flocks of white leghorn hens, or to hear the singing of the orioles as they flitted about near their home-nest, pendent on a branch of a noble, wide-spreading elm, the shade of which he greatly enjoyed. Or perhaps it was to look at redbreast robins familiarly strutting about in the yard, as if proud of their pedestrian feats and thankful that they could dine so near the poplar tree.

Once, when Willie was out but had not been absent more than two or three minutes, his mother followed, looking here and there for the little "runaway." She then called him; but no cooing or prattling could she hear. She ran to the street and looked up and down, without seeing him. Where could he be? She went to the barn, to the carriage-house, to the wood-shed,—but no Willie could she find. Her heart went thump, thump, thump! She went to the garden and orchard, but could nowhere find the darling wee boy.

Had he wandered to the Spicket river? It might be. She looked for his foot-prints, but could find none. She went to the bridge which spans the river a few rods from the house, and looked down into the deep water, but could not discern any trace of the lost child. Back and forth she walked, peering into the water on each side of the bridge, almost breathless from anxiety and fear. What could she do? Where could she go?

She heard an approaching carriage. It brought dear ones returning from church. With sorrow they learned all. Each started on a tour of search, going to the houses of neighbors, from an eighth to a quarter of a mile distant. Willie had not been seen!

The isolation of the house made it probable that, if not drowned, he was somewhere on the farm. The father went up the lane, over the hill, past the woods, by the walnut tree and a lone cedar, standing like a sentinel,—through pastures abounding with flowers, bushes and berries. On, on he went, in a well-beaten track, made by the older children in going to and from school. He often halted and called aloud, "Willie, Willie!" looking in all directions for his dear lost boy without avail.

With increasing anxiety he hastened forward, purposing that a band of men should make a wider search. But, hark! A slight noise, as of a baby when caressed. What is it? Where is it? The father stands still and listens quietly. Again he hears the noise, and, looking and listening intently, he sees among the bushes his own loved Willie, happily playing and prattling, wholly unconscious of having caused such alarm With joyful fleetness he reached and clasped his lost boy, and carried him back to the saddened home, where all were made glad and thankful for the safe return of the innocent little wanderer.

NOTE.—Our first farm home in Salem was pleasantly situated near Policy pond (now Canobic lake). We next lived in the center village, having two or three acres adjoining the buildings and twenty acres a half mile distant. We removed in the spring of 1863 to the large farm, in the southern part of Salem, which was thenceforward our home and was the scene of the incident just described. This is an excellent location for market farming and gardening, as the distance to Lawrence, Mass., is only four miles. The house was long used as a country tavern, before the building of the railroad from Lawrence to Manchester, which crosses the farm. This homestead is now owned and occupied by the son, Jacob William, who was the central figure of the foregoing narrative. On adjoining farms my oldest son, Benjamin, and my daughter Emma live; and my widowed daughter, Esther, and her boys, live with me in the village of Salem Depot, only about two and a half miles distant from the others and their families.

THE RED SCHOOLHOUSE.

Written in 1877, and dedicated to my brothers and sisters.

There, on many a summer day,
We met to study and to play;
There, 'mid winter's drifting snows,
Curling smoke in the air arose.
So, now, meet children there as then,
But there shall we ne'er meet again.

There were planted the seeds for thought;
Have we nourished them as we ought?
Trellis'd and pruned each tender vine,
And taught the tendrils where to twine?
If so, the world now little knows
Who sowed the seed, and first trimmed the rose!

That house, the small red schoolhouse, stands
Where pines and birches grow in the sands;
There may it stand in future days,
Remembered by others to love and praise.
And from its training may Mind and Might
Go forth to live for the Truth and Right.

LEAVES HAVE FALLEN.

The leaves have fallen everywhere;
The trees which were so green, are bare;
Their brighter dress cool Autumn dyed
Red, brown, and golden, glorified!
But who will grieve for fallen leaves,
When have been gathered harvest sheaves?

PUBLISHED WRITINGS OF WARREN UPHAM.

NEW HAMPSHIRE.

In the *Geology of New Hampshire* (three volumes, with atlas; price $25; to be purchased from Arthur H. Chase. state librarian, Concord, N. H.):

History of Explorations among the White Mountains; chapter IV in vol. I, 1874, pp. 59-118, with figures in the text, and views from photographs. Narrative of early and later explorations, with journal of the party. under the direction of Profs. Hitchcock and Huntington. who first spent the winter on Mt. Washington, in 1870-71, for meteorological observations.

River Systems of New Hampshire; chapter XI in the same volume, pp. 298-330. with two maps, and views from photographs.

Modified Drift in New Hampshire: chapter I in vol. III, 1878. pp. 3-176. with seven plates of maps. and 48 figures in the text, mostly sections. Description, and explanation of the origin, of the valley drift terraces, plains, and intervals, in the valleys of the Connecticut, Merrimack, Androscoggin, Saco, and other rivers of this state, formed during the closing part of the Ice age or Glacial period.

The Distribution of the Till: in chapter II of vol. III, pp. 285-309. Description of the lenticular hills of till, since called drumlins, which have a fine development in many tracts of southern New Hampshire: with a view of drumlins in Goffstown, and five map sheets in the atlas, illustrating the glacial geology of the whole state.

Changes in the Relative Heights of Land and Sea during the Glacial and Champlain periods: also in chapter II of this third volume, pp. 329-333.

(Throughout the three volumes of this report and its atlas, the greater part of the drafting of maps and sections was done by Mr. Upham, under the direction of Prof. C. H. Hitchcock, the state geologist.)

In the *Atlas of New Hampshire*, 1877:

The River Systems, pp. 18-21.

Railroads in New Hampshire, pp. 29-31.

MINNESOTA.

In the *Annual Reports of the Geological and Natural History Survey of Minnesota* (distributed on application to Prof. N. H. Winchell, the state geologist, Minneapolis):

Preliminary Report on the Geology of Central and Western Minnesota: Eighth An. Rep., for 1879, pp. 70-125. Descriptions of the bed rocks, and, more in detail, of the glacial and modified drift, with the first notice of beaches of Lake Agassiz. This name was here first proposed for the glacial lake held by the barrier of the waning ice sheet, during the closing stage of the Glacial period, in the valley of the Red river of the North and in the basin of lake Winnipeg.

Report of Progress in Exploration of the Glacial Drift and its Terminal Moraines: Ninth An. Rep., for 1880, pp. 281-356, with plate vi (two maps, and a section across the Coteau des Prairies). The courses of the marginal moraines through Minnesota and Dakota are described and mapped. The two outer moraines pass by Altamont and Gary, S. Dak.; and a part of the third moraine is known as the Antelope hills. From this report of these three localities, our three earliest belts of hilly marginal drift were later named, by Prof. T. C. Chamberlin, the Altamont, Gary, and Antelope moraines.

Notes of Rock-outcrops in Minnesota; Eleventh An. Rep., for 1882, pp. 86-136, with a map.

Lake Agassiz; a chapter in Glacial Geology; do. pp. 137-153, with a map.

Catalogue of the Flora of Minnesota: Twelfth An. Rep., for 1883. Part vi, 193 pages; with a map showing areas of forest and prairie, and approximate limits of some of the principal trees and shrubs. The number of flowering plants known to grow without cultivation in Minnesota, as here catalogued, with notes of their geographic range, is 1,582, with 68 ferns and their allies; in total, 1,650 species.

Notes on the Geology of Minnehaha county, [South] Dakota: Thirteenth An. Rep., for 1884, pp. 88-97, with three figures in the text.

Preliminary Report of Field Work during 1893 in Northeastern Minnesota, chiefly relating to the Glacial Drift; Twenty-second An. Rep., for 1893, pp. 18-66; with sections, and a map of the glacial geology of northern Minnesota.

Late Glacial or Champlain Subsidence and Re-elevation of the St. Lawrence River Basin: Twenty-third An. Rep., for 1894, pp. 156-193; with a map showing the maximum area of the ice-sheet and stages of its recession in the northern United States and southern Canada.

In the *Final Reports of the Geological and Natural History Survey of Minnesota* (for sale, on application to Prof. N. H. Winchell, the state geologist, Minneapolis, the price of each volume being $3.50 in cloth binding, or $5 in half leather): vol. i, 1884, ten chapters (xii-xvii, and xix-xxii), pp. 404-532, and 562-647, with ten maps, describing seventeen counties in southern Minnesota: and vol. II, 1888, twenty chapters (IV-X, and XIV-XXVI), pp. 102-263, and 309-671, with twenty maps, describing thirty-three counties in eastern, central, and western Minnesota.

THE UNITED STATES.

Published by the *United States Geological Survey* (for sale, on application to the Director of this Survey, Washington, D. C.):

The Upper Beaches and Deltas of the Glacial Lake Agassiz; Bulletin No. 39. 1887, 84 pages, with a map; price, 10 cents.

Altitudes between Lake Superior and the Rocky Mountains; Bulletin No. 72, 1891, 229 pages; price 20 cents. Tabulation of altitudes determined by railroad surveys in northern Wisconsin, northern Iowa, Minnesota, South and North Dakota, northern Nebraska, and Montana; along the Northern Pacific railroad beyond the Rocky Mountains to the Pacific coast; and the Canadian Pacific Railway system from Port Arthur to the Pacific.

The Glacial Lake Agassiz: Monograph XXV, 1895: quarto, xxiv and 658 pages, with 38 plates (mostly maps), and 35 figures in the text (mostly sections and profiles); price, $1.70. A full description of lake Agassiz, which attained a length of nearly 700 miles, a maximum width of more than 200 miles, and an area of 110,000 square miles or more, being thus larger than the combined areas of the five great lakes tributary to the St. Lawrence river. By a differential continental uplift, which was in progress and nearly completed during the departure of the ice-sheet, the shore lines of this lake were inclined, so that the earliest and highest shore has an ascent of about 400 feet in a distance of 400 miles northward from the southern end and outlet of the lake. Besides the description of the evidences of this ancient lake, and discussion of its relations to the receding ice-sheet, other chapters treat of the bed-rocks of the region, of its artesian and common wells, and of the agricultural resources of the Red River Valley, which is the most fertile wheat-raising district of North America.

CANADA.

Published by the *Geological Survey of Canada* (for sale, on application to the Director of this Survey, Ottawa, Canada): Report of Exploration of the Glacial Lake Agassiz in Manitoba; in the Annual Report of this Survey, new series, vol. IV, for 1888-89, forming Part E, 156 pages, with two maps and a plate of sections; price, for this part separately, 25 cents, or for the entire volume (published both in English and in French), $2. Four-fifths of the area of lake Agassiz were north of the international boundary, reaching to the present Saskatchewan and Nelson rivers.

THE MINNESOTA HISTORICAL SOCIETY.

In the *Minnesota Historical Society Collections*, vol. viii. pp. 11-24: The Settlement and Development of the Red River Valley. This paper, with others by Dr. U. S. Grant and Prof. N. H. Winchell, form Part I of this volume, issued in 1895 (40 pages, with a map of northern Minnesota); price 25 cents, on application to the secretary of the society, St. Paul.

OTHER BOOKS.

The Ice Age in North America, and its bearings upon the Antiquity of Man. By G. Frederick Wright. With an Appendix (pp. 573-595) on the " *Probable Causes of Glaciation,*" by Warren Upham. Pages xviii and 622, with numerous maps, views from photographs, and other illustrations, including 143 figures in the text. New York: D. Appleton & Co., 1889. Price, $5. In 1896 the fourth edition of this work was issued, with a preface (pages v-xxv) by Prof. Wright, including bibliographic lists of the principal American contributions to glacial geology during the preceding five years. Thirty-nine titles of papers by Mr. Upham are here noted.

Greenland Icefields and Life in the North Atlantic, with a new discussion of the Causes of the Ice Age. By G. Frederick Wright and Warren Upham. Pages xv and 407, with five inset maps and 66 figures in the text. New York: D. Appleton & Co., 1896. Price, $2. The maps were drafted, and chapters viii to xiv (pp. 188-361) were written, by Mr. Upham. The titles of these chapters are: viii. The Plants of Greenland; ix. The Animals of Greenland; x. Explorations of the Inland Ice of Greenland; xi. Comparison of Pleistocene and Present Ice-sheets; xii. Pleistocene Changes of Level around the Basin of the North Atlantic; xiii. The Causes of the Ice Age; xiv. Stages of the Ice Age in North America and Europe.

It is thought that the Ice Age was caused chiefly by great uplifts of the lands which were glaciated and drift-covered, giving them so high altitude that they received frequent snowfalls throughout the year, by which ice-sheets were formed to the thickness of thousands of feet. The depths of fjords and continuations of river valleys on the submerged borders of North America and Europe indicate that their maximum vertical extent of uplift was 3,000 to 5,000 feet, or more, above their present levels. These continental areas then became enveloped by ice-sheets whose surface in the central part was probably about two miles above the sea level, like the ice-sheet which now covers the interior of Greenland. Under the great weight of the accumulated ice, however, the lands sank until they lay mostly somewhat lower than now during the closing part or Champlain epoch of the Ice Age, as is known by fossiliferous marine beds on many areas near the coast, overlying the till and other drift deposits. When the borders of the ice-sheet were thus depressed from their formerly high altitude, warmer climatic conditions caused them to be rapidly melted away.

SHORTER PAPERS.

Numerous papers, mostly on glacial geology, in the Proceedings
of the American Association for the Advancement of Science, for 1876,
and onward; in Appalachia, published by the Appalachian Mountain
Club, 1876, and onward: the American Naturalist. Sept., 1877, and onward: the American Journal of Science, Dec., 1877, and onward; the
Canadian Naturalist, 1878: the Proceedings of the Boston Society of
Natural History, for 1879, and onward; the Bulletin of the Minnesota
Academy of Natural Sciences (1882-); the American Geologist, of Minneapolis (1888-); the Geological Magazine, of London (1889-); the Bulletin of the Geological Society of America (1890-): the Popular Science
Monthly, Sept., 1891, and onward: the Journal of the Victoria Insti-
tute, of London (1892-); Science, 1893; the Glacialists' Magazine, of
Leeds, England, 1893, and onward; and the Journal of Geology, of Chi-
cago, 1894, and onward.

The Catalogue and Index of Contributions to North American Geology,
1732-1891, by N. H. Darton (Bulletin No. 127, of the U. S. Geological
Survey, 1896), gives, in pages 966-969, sixty titles of Mr. Upham's papers and reports. These titles and those of later years given in the new
edition of the Ice Age in North America, before mentioned, constitute
a nearly complete list to the present time.

EDITORIAL WORK.

Many reviews, contributed as one of the editors of the American Geologist and of the Glacialists' Magazine, during the past five years.

THE AMERICAN GEOLOGIST is a monthly magazine, founded in 1888,
published by a board of twelve editors.   Each year has two volumes of
more than 400 pages each, with portraits, maps, and figures in the text.
Subscriptions ($3.50 yearly) and orders for back numbers, which can be
supplied from the beginning, should be addressed to Prof. N. H.
Winchell, Minneapolis, Minn.

THE GLACIALISTS' MAGAZINE is a British quarterly journal of Glacial
Geology, founded in 1893, edited by Prof. Percy F. Kendall (of Chapel
Allerton, Leeds, England) and Warren Upham.   Each year has a vol-
ume of about 200 pages, with maps and other illustrations.   The yearly
subscription is six shillings ($1.50): address Arthur R. Dwerryhouse, 65
Louis street, Leeds, England.

INDEX.

www.ingramcontent.com/pod-product-compliance
Lightning Source LLC
Chambersburg PA
CBHW021521090426

42739CB00007B/716